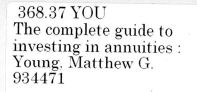

D0767798

The Complete Guide to Investing in Annuities

How to Earn High Rates of Return Safely

By Matthew G. Young

THE COMPLETE GUIDE TO INVESTING IN ANNUITIES: HOW TO EARN HIGH RATES OF RETURN SAFELY

Copyright © 2011 Atlantic Publishing Group, Inc.
1405 SW 6th Avenue • Ocala, Florida 34471 • Phone 800-814-1132 • Fax 352-622-1875
Web site: www.atlantic-pub.com • E-mail: sales@atlantic-pub.com
SAN Number: 268-1250

Library of Congress Cataloging-in-Publication Data

Young, Matthew G.
 The complete guide to investing in annuities : how to earn high rates of return safely / by Matthew G Young.
    p. cm.
 Includes bibliographical references and index.
 ISBN-13: 978-1-60138-291-7 (alk. paper)
 ISBN-10: 1-60138-291-X (alk. paper)
 1. Annuities. 2. Variable annuities. 3. Rate of return. 4. Investments. I. Title.

 HG8790.Y68 2010
 368.3'7--dc22
                                        2010005094

PEER REVIEWER • Marilee Griffin • PROJECT MANAGER : Nicole Orr
PROOFREADER: Brett Daly • brett.daly1@gmail.com
FRONT COVER DESIGN: Meg Buchner • meg@megbuchner.com
BACK COVER DESIGN: Jackie Miller • millerjackiej@gmail.com

Printed on Recycled Paper

Printed in the United States

A few years back we lost our beloved pet dog Bear, who was not only our best and dearest friend but also the "Vice President of Sunshine" here at Atlantic Publishing. He did not receive a salary but worked tirelessly 24 hours a day to please his parents.

Bear was a rescue dog who turned around and showered myself, my wife, Sherri, his grandparents Jean, Bob, and Nancy, and every person and animal he met (well, maybe not rabbits) with friendship and love. He made a lot of people smile every day.

We wanted you to know a portion of the profits of this book will be donated in Bear's memory to local animal shelters, parks, conservation organizations, and other individuals and nonprofit organizations in need of assistance.

– Douglas & Sherri Brown

PS: We have since adopted two more rescue dogs: first Scout, and the following year, Ginger. They were both mixed golden retrievers who needed a home.

Want to help animals and the world? Here are a dozen easy suggestions you and your family can implement today:

- *Adopt and rescue a pet from a local shelter.*
- *Support local and no-kill animal shelters.*
- *Plant a tree to honor someone you love.*
- *Be a developer — put up some birdhouses.*
- *Buy live, potted Christmas trees and replant them.*
- *Make sure you spend time with your animals each day.*
- *Save natural resources by recycling and buying recycled products.*
- *Drink tap water, or filter your own water at home.*
- *Whenever possible, limit your use of or do not use pesticides.*
- *If you eat seafood, make sustainable choices.*
- *Support your local farmers market.*
- *Get outside. Visit a park, volunteer, walk your dog, or ride your bike.*

Five years ago, Atlantic Publishing signed the Green Press Initiative. These guidelines promote environmentally friendly practices, such as using recycled stock and vegetable-based inks, avoiding waste, choosing energy-efficient resources, and promoting a no-pulping policy. We now use 100-percent recycled stock on all our books. The results: in one year, switching to post-consumer recycled stock saved 24 mature trees, 5,000 gallons of water, the equivalent of the total energy used for one home in a year, and the equivalent of the greenhouse gases from one car driven for a year.

Acknowledgements

I dedicate this book to the two most influential males in my life: my father, Robert, and my son, Ethan.

There are several individuals who contributed to the making of this book in some fashion or another. It would be incomplete and unfair to not mention the help that was provided and to thank those who lent me their time, insight, and expertise.

Thank you to Kerri Eames for her proofreading and suggestions during the formative stages of this book.

Thank you to my case studies: Colleen, Richard, Jim, David, Rick, Joel, Ted, and Rob.

Thank you to my amazing editors: Nicole and Marilee. You never let me settle for mediocre writing or ideas.

And last but certainly not least, thank you to my family, especially Beth, my wife, who has been infinitely patient with me.

Table of Contents

CHAPTER 2: Making Annuities Work for You   37

CHAPTER 3: Annuity Misconceptions   61

CHAPTER 4: Fixed Annuities   75

CHAPTER 5: Variable Annuities   85

The Complete Guide to Investing in Annuities

CHAPTER 6: Equity-indexed Annuities   111

CHAPTER 7: Tax-sheltered Annuities   125

CHAPTER 8: Product Features   135

CHAPTER 9: Subtypes of Annuities   143

CHAPTER 15: Questions to Ask Your Agent 213

CHAPTER 16: Structuring Your Annuity 221

CHAPTER 17: The Future of Annuities 235

The Complete Guide to Investing in Annuities

Introduction

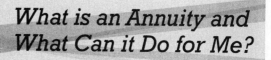

What is an Annuity and What Can it Do for Me?

Annuities may seem overwhelming at first, and for a good reason. There are many different types and even more add-ons that allow investors to customize their investment. On the surface, annuities are a complex investment, but they can be extremely beneficial, if you have a plan. This section is meant to introduce you to the world of annuities and give you an overview of what is in store for the rest of the book. If you feel overwhelmed, do not worry. There is a glossary of technical terms included at the end of this book. If you come across a term you do not know, feel free to look it up. Additionally, there is a series of appendices containing easy-to-use charts, glossaries, and other information that will ease the decision-making process.

A Brief Overview of Annuities and How They Can Help You Retire Safely

An annuity is a contract between an investor looking for stable returns and an insurance company. Although an understanding of annuities obviously requires a deeper look than this, annuities are not nearly as complicated as they may seem on the surface. They are rich in potential for investors planning out their futures.

My intent with the following pages is to give you an in-depth look at what annuities are, how they work, and why they should be a part of your retirement portfolio. I also include several tips and things to look for when determining which annuity product features are right for you.

The basic concept of an annuity is similar to any investment product: You put money into it in order to have it grow in value so that when the money is withdrawn at a later date, there is more. Annuities are much like Certificates of Deposit (CD), an investment contract with a bank for a set period, or Money Market Accounts (MMA), which are a higher interest savings account linked to a market's performance, in this respect, except that they are tax-deferred as they grow. This actually makes annuities, over time, much more valuable than a CD or MMA. But, there are other differences that still make it worthwhile to hold these other investment products. Although an annuity is a great investment choice, it may not cover all of your financial needs. Annuities are, for the most part, not meant as short-term investments. Money market accounts, and even savings accounts, are much better tools for this purpose.

The main reason to own an annuity is security. Annuities are an insurance product and do help you to ensure a more rewarding retirement. In addition to this, many annuities are guaranteed for a minimum rate of return, and in good market times, some companies may even increase the amount returned to investors. Annuities are designed to give you a steady and consistent return on your investment. There are even options that will give you this steady source of income for the rest of your life.

Predictability is another key feature. Fixed annuities have a set minimum interest rate so investors know exactly how much money they will have five, ten, or even 20 years down the road. For retirees on a fixed income, this peace of mind is very reassuring.

Many companies have scaled back the benefits provided to retirees; pensions and company-matched **401(k)s** are becoming a thing of the past, and annuities are becoming more popular. What used to appear as safeguards for retirees are no longer their best options. In order to have a reliable source of income for your senior years, something more is necessary. Retirees have been compelled to look elsewhere.

With these things in mind, start to explore how an annuity can help maximize your capital during your retirement years.

The scenario

You are reaching retirement age and have built a sizeable nest egg. You want to maximize the gains you will see, and what is more, you want to preserve that nest egg. What options do you have? A mutual fund, where your investment is at the mercy of the market, or perhaps a money market account or a CD, where you will see only minimal gains on your investment. What other choices are out there?

If you are getting near retirement age and want to do some planning, and, like the person in the previous scenario, you want to preserve your assets and maximize your returns, an annuity is the perfect investment for you. Annuities are much more predictable and stable than the stock market, yet they offer higher returns than the typical financial products offered by banks. An annuity, in conjunction with these products, can provide you with a fruitful retirement. If you are currently planning for your retirement, or if you will be at some point in the distant future, this book is for you. Annuities are flexible enough to serve the needs of almost anyone who wants a secure future.

Annuities are also beneficial to the younger population. Even if you do not have much in the way of savings, an annuity may be just what you are looking for. Variable annuities, when contributed to regularly over a long period, can be extremely beneficial to an investor because they offer returns that fluctuate on the stock market's performance.

The players

There are a few key people you should know about. The first is the annuity **owner**. This is the person who signs the contract and pays premiums into it. This individual has all of the rights that come with owning an annuity, including the decision-making process regarding premium payments and desired time frames. The owner is normally, but not always, the **annuitant**. The annuitant is the one who receives distributions from the annuity. This is not to be confused with the **beneficiary** named within the contract. Beneficiaries are the people who receive annuity funds, if there are any, upon the death of the annuitant.

On the other end of the sales process is the **agent** or **broker**. This is the woman or man who sells annuities. They may represent one insurance company or be an independent agent with the ability to sell many companies' products. Agents may receive a salary or work solely off commission. In order to sell fixed and equity-indexed annuities, the agent must have a current life insurance license within the state they conduct business. For variable annuities, an additional securities license is mandatory because variable annuities fluctuate in price in accordance with the stock market. This license is mandated by the Financial Industry Regulatory Authority (FINRA).

How Annuities Work

Annuities have two phases: the **accumulation phase**, where money is put into the annuity and gains interest; and the **annuitization (or payout) phase**, where money is distributed out of the annuity to the annuitant. Annuities are funded by an investor over a course of time, tailored to his or her choosing. As mentioned before, this is called the accumulation phase. This can be done with a one-time **premium** — or payment — over the course of many years, or any period deemed appropriate. Interest is earned in a compound fashion during the accumulation phase, meaning the interest earned over a specific period will accumulate its own interest.

Once the accumulation period is over, the annuitization period begins. This is when the investor, the individual placing his or her money into an annuity, begins to see money return to him or her. Annuities are taxed on a **last in, first out basis**, meaning that the principal amount is not taxed, merely the interest gained. This money is taxable first, leaving the principal amount, which is withdrawn in later installments, tax-free. This is due to the fact that annuities are normally purchased with post-tax dollars. Pre-tax, or qualified annuities, however, are treated a bit differently.

It may surprise you to learn that most annuitants do not go through with the annuitization of their contract. Instead, they make systematic draws from their accounts like they would from another retirement product. Although this gives investors easier access to their money, it may not be in their best interest. As you will see, annuities, if properly used, can have a profound impact on an investor's retirement. Features, such as a guaranteed income for life, are only available to those who annuitize their contract.

This is a cause of contention among investment experts. What is better: easy access to your money or a guarantee that you will never run out of money? This is not a question that can be answered easily. The answer will vary from person to person and will even vary for the same person over a given period.

What makes annuities worthwhile investments?

Even though annuities are not Federal Deposit Insurance Corporation (FDIC) insured products, they are guaranteed by the companies that sell them. If you are worried about the lack of a government guarantee, there are rating services that evaluate the fiscal strength of insurance companies. Moody's Investors Service, Standard & Poor's, and A.M. Best are three of the most popular rating agencies.

But, even though annuities are not federally guaranteed products, there are still many safeguards that exist in order to protect your investment. Strength ratings are one way in which consumers are protected. These ratings help investors gauge the financial solvency of the company they entrust their money to. Another protection is the fact that each state has similar laws protecting the solvency of insurance companies. Most states have safeguards in place that protect investments up to $100,000, while other states, such as New York, go up to $500,000. This guarantee is made by each state's Guaranty Association, an organization that protects policyholders from poorly managed insurance companies. Although it is illegal for an insurance company to advertise that they belong to the Guaranty Association in the majority of states, membership is a prerequisite for doing business in that state. Therefore, businesses, including insurance companies, cannot run their practices without being a member, which ultimately works to your benefit as the investor. *For a complete list of the amounts guaranteed per state and each state's stipulations, see Appendix A.*

Most annuities offer rates superior to Certificates of Deposit or Money Market Accounts. Because of this, annuities are growing in popularity among investors looking for safe returns, especially retirees, and those approaching retirement age who do not want to take risks with their money.

Annuities offer stability that the stock market cannot match, making them a valuable part of a retiree's portfolio. While the stock market may drop in value, most annuities are guaranteed products. True, an annuity may not see some of the dramatic increases that the stock market sees, but they are a way to avoid the natural, and sometimes harsh, fluctuations of the ever-changing market. This makes them the perfect choice for those who want stability in their portfolios. Annuities can do this because the insurance company acts as a middleman between the investment and the customer. In other words, the insurance company manages the money rather than the annuitant, or the investor. The annuitant has a say in variable annuities as to which types of funds his or her money is put into, but it is ultimately the insurance company that oversees the funds.

There are a plethora of other advantages in owning annuities. Annuities offer professionally managed funds without the high commission charges that mutual funds carry. There are also ways to withdraw your money without added penalties or fees. Perhaps the characteristic that makes an annuity the most worthwhile investment for some is that they have a guaranteed death benefit to a beneficiary that avoids probate. If the annuity you are in is not performing well, there are always tax-free exchanges available to you, assuming you are still in the accumulation phase. These exchanges are known as the industry as Section 1035 exchanges. *See Chapter 12 for more details.*

Who benefits most from annuities?

There are a few different classes of people who will benefit from investing in annuities. The first class of individuals are those in higher tax brackets. Because annuity earnings are counted as income, a problem is created for people on the brink of a higher tax bracket. It would push their earnings up, ultimately forcing them to pay more in taxes in the long run. For example, assume you earn $82,000 per year and are a single filer. By delaying the income that your annuity earns until after retirement, you avoid jumping up to the next tax bracket. In 2010, the 25 percent tax bracket was capped at $82,400. The extra $400 is an amount that a good mutual fund should certainly surpass in a year. Because the earnings are delayed, the annuitant has the ability to stay in the 25 percent bracket and pay a lower tax rate than if he or she was in the next highest tax bracket, where an extra 3 percent of earnings has to be paid.

Thanks to the benefits of **tax deferral**, annuities are a great way of relieving short-term tax burdens. Large annuity earnings do not have to be reported until the money is withdrawn at retirement when the investor is normally in a lower tax bracket because of having a new, lower income, or sometimes because of having a fixed income.

Those who have maximized contributions into qualified retirement accounts, such as IRAs and Roth IRAs, also benefit. These investments are made with pre-tax dollars but act much like variable annuities. There is no limit to how much you can deposit into an annuity though, while IRAs and Roth IRAs both have limits. There is also no maximum amount you can earn in a year in order to contribute, such as with Roth IRAs where an investor can only earn up to $105,000 in a single year if he or she is a single filer on income taxes. Starting in 2010, it should be noted that there is no earning cap for conversions from a traditional IRA to a Roth IRA. There will still be earning regulations regarding the outright purchase of a Roth IRA though, which will keep annuities competitive in the investing marketplace.

Investors with long-term retirement plans will also benefit. Annuities are a great way to save money for your later years because you cannot easily access annuity funds until you reach retirement age. In this regard, annuities act much like a chaperoned investing plan.

Annuities and You

This book is designed to help you determine whether the purchase of an annuity is right for you. In most cases, the answer to this question will be yes. In that case, this book will help you determine which kind of annuity will work best for your needs and goals, while considering age, financial status, and other important variables. This book will also help you determine which features will benefit you the most. Do not be afraid if all of this seems complicated at first; this book is designed to make it easy for you to comprehend it all. With that said, annuities are a great addition to retirement portfolios. This book will allow you to understand the ins and outs of annuities and ease your decision-making process. It is truly important that you find a product that matches your needs. Annuities offer the flexibility to meet those needs, regardless of what stage you are at in your life.

Why annuities?

Annuities exist because of security. They offer steady and consistent gains that cannot be outlived. The only other benefit programs that offer this are social security and company pensions, which are decreasing rapidly. Even social security is scaling back; 2010 is the first year in decades that benefits have not increased.

Annuities act in two stages. The first of these is when capital is accumulated. While you are in the accumulation phase, your money grows tax-deferred. For example, assume you have an initial $10,000 to invest into an annuity. After the first year, you can contribute $500 per year into the annuity until you reach retirement age. If you start at age 30, and contribute up to age 64, counting the entire first year and the entire last year, that is a total of 35 years you will contribute into the annuity during your working years, for a total of $17,500. With an 8 percent rate of return, you can expect to have $135,921 left in a taxable account, assuming you are in the 25 percent tax bracket. For 2010, the 25 percent tax bracket was for those who earned between $34,000.01-$82,400 for single filers and between $68,000 and $137,300 for joint filers.

Now, assume you start investing the same $500 per year at age 30 again, except you choose to invest in a tax-deferred annuity. With all other factors being equal, the total amount you have when you turn 65 will be $240,904. That is more than a $100,000 difference. By this point, you will be retired and in a lower tax bracket. Assuming you are now in the 15 percent bracket, instead of the 25 percent bracket, you will still have $208,893 at your disposal. To figure out your own customized tax-deferred investment, visit KJE Computer Solutions' website at **www.dinkytown.net/java/FixedAnnuity.html**. This site includes more than 350 financial calculators, all aimed at helping you structure your retirement and other aspects of your financial life.

The second stage involves annuitizing your investment. This is where you will start receiving distributions back from the insurance company. Not all annuities need to be annuitized.

Remember, the longer the money is left in a tax-deferred account, the more advantageous it will be. Retirement accounts were given tax-deferred status in order to encourage people to invest in them. Use this to your advantage. Tax deferral however, should not be confused with tax exemption. Although some municipal securities, such as government bonds, have tax-free earnings, annuities do not. You will pay taxes on your annuity eventually; tax deferral is the most advantageous way to pay these.

Annuities are tools to fight the problems that come along with retirement as well. Once you retire, the Social Security check you receive will not be as large of a source of income as your paycheck from your employer was. If properly used, annuities can cover this balance and allow you to live the lifestyle you always dreamed of for your retirement years.

An annuity can simplify your life, too. Rather than having to closely manage your retirement money, you allow another entity to take over this task and manage it for you. Money management can be a labor-intensive undertaking. By allowing the insurance company to take care of everything for you, you can spend your time doing the things you enjoy. After all, is that not what retirement is all about?

Chapter 1

What Differentiates Annuities from Other Financial Products?

nnuities are similar in some aspects to many other financial products. In other aspects, they are completely different. They may have time limits like CDs. They also may be connected to the stock market like a mutual fund. These similarities should not be seen as confusing but as something that allows you to gain a deeper understanding of how they work. All financial products have their benefits and disadvantages. Annuities are no different. Annuities, however, offer more benefits than any other financial product out there when it comes to planning for a retirement.

Annuities

An **annuity** is a contract between a person and an insurance company, such as Prudential Financial, Inc. or State Farm Insurance, with the primary purpose of giving retirees a permanent source of income they cannot outlive. No other financial product can boast this. Premiums, the amount of money you put into the annuity, can consist of one single lump sum payment or multiple smaller payments, known as **flexible premiums**. Although considered an insurance product, annuities actually have only some elements in common with insurance, the most prevalent being a probate-free death benefit. **Probate** is a court process that an individual's estate goes through after he or she dies, and it can last between six months and two years. All of the deceased individual's assets are completely frozen during this process, including savings and any other investments. Because annuities are an insurance product, sold by a life insurance agent, they bypass probate. Rather than being part of the court procedures, heirs receive annuity money immediately, just like they would with any other life insurance product. This death benefit is considered by some to be one of the best features of an annuity.

Nonetheless, annuities are more of an investment than an insurance product. Because annuities are geared toward retirees, they can only be accessed after the annuitant reaches the age 59½. Withdrawals prior to this are taxed with a 10 percent penalty.

An annuity can be further broken into two subcategories: fixed or variable. **Fixed annuities** offer a guaranteed minimum rate of return, while **variable annuities** offer returns that will fluctuate with the stock market's performance. These variable returns are often connected with the performance of a **market index**, a group of stocks bunched together to gauge the overall strength of the market, such as the Standard & Poor's 500.

Another major feature of annuities is they grow tax-deferred, a key feature among other retirement products, such as 401(k)s and IRAs. This does not mean that annuities are tax-free, though. Rather than being taxed on a yearly basis like other investments, annuities are only taxed once withdrawals begin.

Annuities are complex and oftentimes difficult to understand. This book will act as a resource for you to fully understand annuities and how they can help you meet your needs in a manner that other financial products cannot.

One benefit an annuity has over other investment products is the right to revoke your money if you are unhappy with your decision. This revocation may occur only during the free look period, which is normally 30 days. Other investments, especially CDS, require you to pay a penalty if you decide to withdraw your money earlier than the terms you agreed upon.

Certificates of Deposit

Certificates of Deposit allow investors to put money into an account for a specified amount of time, and in return, offer a small rate of return that is guaranteed by the federal government. There is a penalty if you withdraw the money before the specified amount of time has passed. These time limits can range from a few months to a few years.

Like a CD, an annuity allows investors to put a sum of money into an account for a fixed amount of time. This does not have to be one lump-sum payment like a CD, and while it is guaranteed by the company that backs it, it is not FDIC insured. Also, like a CD, there is a penalty if money is withdrawn prior to the time parameters established. Annuities are normally, but not necessarily, investments for longer periods than a CD; there are **immediate annuities** that begin payouts in less than a year, although immediate annuities are not as common as deferred annuities. Immediate annuities are not quite as popular because they necessitate a large premium upfront, something that many people cannot afford. Deferred annuities, on the other hand, can be used to fund a retirement after sometimes many years of paying premiums into them.

Although CDs are held for a period of six months to five years, most deferred annuities are kept for at least ten years or more. In fact, deferred annuities may give their annuitant a penalty if funds are withdrawn too soon. Also, gains made by CDs are subject to current capital gains taxation rates each year, while annuities grow tax-deferred. Both a CD and an annuity are stable investments that appeal to retirees.

Money Market Accounts

Money market accounts are higher-interest savings accounts that can also be used in the same manner as a checking account. Banks require high balances for this type of account in order to avoid maintenance fees. They do offer more **liquidity** of your funds than an annuity typically will because you can debit your account with checks or a debit card at your own discretion.

MMAs are great for keeping large amounts of money for a short-term period but do not perform as well as a longer-term investment. Annuities offer a much more competitive rate of return over the long haul, even when you take into account the occasional losses that a variable annuity may face. MMAs do act as a great place to stash emergency money, though. In other words, if you are trying to plan for a retirement, a MMA alone will not suffice. It may, however, eventually play a part in your retirement portfolio because they allow much easier access to your money. In fact, some MMAs even allow you to use the funds as a checking account, something that annuities cannot do. However, annuities do offer higher historical rates of return. There is a distinct trade-off between ease of access to your money and the rate of return.

Mutual Funds

Mutual funds are groups of pooled monies that can be comprised of stocks, bonds, indices, and other investment products. A fund manager who groups many investors' capital together in order to gain more equity closely oversees these funds. In this respect, they closely mirror variable annuities.

Mutual funds are not guaranteed to make the investor money. In fact, mutual funds often lose money because they fluctuate with the stock market. When the market sours, so do the majority of mutual funds. There are also high commission charges and maintenance fees associated with mutual funds.

Mutual funds can be cashed out whenever the investor deems necessary. Annuities must follow certain stipulations set forth in their contract regarding withdrawals — or else they face a penalty. But, there are ways around these penalties.

Like mutual funds, the amount of **principal** invested in a variable annuity is put into a collective fund where it is invested in stocks, bonds, indices, mortgages, and other investments. These funds are overseen by the company's investment manager and vary from company to company. With variable annuities, the investor has much more discretion over where his or her money is invested than an investor of a fixed annuity does. Mutual funds are also subject to current capital gains taxes, while annuities are not.

Exchange Traded Funds

Exchange traded funds (ETFs) are basket funds of like-minded companies that have soared in popularity over the last several years. A basket fund is simply a group of similar business stocks. For instance, a group of biotechnology companies might be included in the same ETF. Because they consist of smaller groups of companies, ETFs are oftentimes much more volatile than the overall market. All ETFs are included in the mutual fund family.

With an immediate variable annuity, you can choose to have an ETF as a higher-risk subaccount. Immediate annuities are annuities in which you will withdraw money before the end of one year. Because these products are unstable, they are usually used by short-term **traders** rather than investors. Both fixed and variable annuities offer a much higher degree of stability than an ETF will give you. If you are looking for a long-term investment, ETFs are not for you. Furthermore, ETFs are not actively managed by a fund manager. It is up to the trader to know if and when to enter or exit a **position** with ETFs. This is just another reason why long-term investors should steer clear of this type of product.

IRAs and Roth IRAs

An **Individual Retirement Account** is a great investment, whether it be a traditional IRA or a Roth IRA (named after their main legislative sponsor, the late Sen. William Roth). The biggest difference between these is the method used by the IRS when it comes to taxes. Traditional IRA contributions are tax deductible, while Roth IRAs are not. IRAs have mandatory withdrawal ages at 70 ½, while Roth IRAs have no mandatory withdrawals. Roth IRAs also have a maximum amount of money, which you can earn yearly. In 2009, the cap amount was $105,000 for single filers wishing to contribute the maximum amount to their Roth IRA. Only earned income can be placed in a Roth IRA — capital gains are ineligible.

It is a little known fact that you can actually convert your current IRA or Roth IRA into an annuity that functions as an IRA or Roth IRA tax-free. Some IRAs are annuities; some are not. Think of this as if the annuity were a vehicle and the IRA the driver. The driver is still subject to the laws that govern IRAs, while the annuity works like other products of its kind.

The age limit for penalties regarding early withdrawal is the same between traditional IRAs and annuities: 59 ½.

401(k) and 403(b) Plans

These are retirement accounts set up through an employer. The numbers and letters that entitle these investments refer to the section and subsection within the Internal Revenue Code in which these plans are established. The IRS's website explains these plans and how they work in greater detail at **www.irs.gov/businesses/small**. Normally, the employer will contribute a matching amount up to a certain limit if you meet the vesting requirements. This may be a certain age or a period of years that you must work for the company.

These are great retirement investments and, if available through your employer, you should contribute at least what your employer matches into these funds if you can. For example, assume your employer will match up to 5 percent of your paycheck, meaning your employer will essentially give you 5 percent of your paycheck as long as you invest 5 percent, too. If you are paid $1,000 each pay cycle, you will want to contribute $50 so the 5 percent threshold is met. In return, your employer will also contribute $50 for a total of $100 each payday. If you wish to contribute more than $50, the employer will not pay more, thus making extra payments into your retirement plan not quite as valuable.

Contributions to these savings plans are made with pre-tax dollars, which makes them tax deductible. Employee-sponsored retirement programs often work just like variable annuities. It is up to you to decide the degree of risk you can tolerate with your investment and decide what percentage of funds you want in which **risk class**. For example, you may want to allocate some of your money in conservative funds and some in more aggressive funds. These risk classes allow you to match your needs to your money's performance. However, like IRAs and annuities, these retirement vessels have a minimum withdrawal age of 59 ½, at which you will not incur a penalty.

403(b) plans, by definition, are annuities. Also called tax-sheltered annuities, 403(b)s are considered qualified plans because they are bought with pre-tax dollars. These plans were created in order to encourage people to save for re-

tirement directly with their employment income. Oftentimes, employers will match the funds put into these accounts.

Stocks and Bonds

Stocks are the most prominently traded financial product
in the U.S. The hectic New York Stock Exchange is perhaps
the most widely known trading venue, where traders shout
out their orders over the roar of the crowd. All this aside, a
stock represents partial ownership of a larger corporation.
Again, you can choose to have parts of your variable annuity in the stock market. An annuity, however, is merely
an investment vehicle where your money is set aside with
the hopes that it will grow into a much larger amount of
money. Stocks and bonds are oftentimes bought by the insurance company you decide to invest your money with if
you buy a fixed annuity, but, in either case, an annuity by
no means gives you the rights and risks associated with
stock and bond ownership. It should be noted that a bond
does not represent ownership in a corporation; it is merely
an amount borrowed by the company to be repaid, plus
interest, at a later date. Variable annuities are titled so because their rate of return varies depending on the market
they are connected to.

Most annuities that are connected to the stock market are
associated with an **index**, a measuring stick of multiple
stocks. When the stocks within an index rise, the index
rises in value, thus making the annuity connected to the
index rise as well. *See Chapter 5 for more information about
variable annuities.*

The Stock Market

The stock market offers huge returns on your investment — if you invest in the right companies. Stocks are a great investment if you can handle the emotional or financial risk associated with them. As people age and their investment goals change, the ratio of money kept in the **stock market** should also change. For a young professional just beginning his or her career, it is appropriate to invest in high-risk products, such as stocks and funds that reflect stock growth, because of the alluring returns. The market has historically offered a competitive rate of return over long periods so if the market bottoms out and the investor loses a good portion of his or her savings, all is not lost. The career of a young professional is just beginning, meaning the earning potential of that individual is still very high. It may take a few years to rebuild what has been lost, but he or she can still recoup from the loss.

This is not the case with retirees, however, who are normally on fixed incomes. A dip in the stock market could result in the worst kind of disaster: an individual outliving their money. This is a fear many senior citizens live with on a daily basis. Although an annuity is not a catch-all solution to this, it can eliminate some of the financial stress associated with aging. Stability is a necessity for people living on fixed incomes; annuities can provide this.

This is not meant to dissuade you from investing in the stock market. The stock market is the backbone of our country's economic stability and is a valuable weapon in any investor's arsenal, but you should invest in products that will fulfill the goals you have set forth for yourself. If a stable and consistent stream of income is important, stock market investments should be put on the backburner.

Safety

Annuities provide safety to annuitants and annuity owners with a multitude of preventative measures. With strict investment procedures and other safeguards, insurance companies have it in their best interest to make your money grow. There are, however, a few other safeguards that need more explanation. These include:

- State guaranty funds

- Holding companies

- Reinsurance

Take a look at each of these three points individually.

State Guaranty Funds: Each state has a guaranty association that insurance companies are required to be members of by law. These associations monitor the fiscal **solvency** of the companies within the state. If a company appears to be in trouble monetarily, the association can step in and rectify the problem. It is illegal for insurance companies to advertise that they belong to a guaranty association because it may create a false impression that they are endorsed by the association.

Holding Companies: Insurance companies will take the money given to them through collected premiums and invest it. This is how their profits grow and how your annuity increases in value. With holding companies, insurance companies add a layer of protection to their investments.

The term "holding company" actually incorporates two different concepts. The first refers to when the insurance company invests its money into other companies. These are normally large corporations that have established themselves as being consistent. Both stocks and bonds are purchased by the insurance company to create a well-balanced portfolio.

The second meaning refers to the umbrella structure that many corporations, and especially insurance companies, form. Some companies have ownership within other companies, loosely affiliating them. The parent company structure is one of the less-complicated versions of a holding company. With this, there is a company that owns enough shares of another company to give it a controlling position within its board of directors.

This is most easily illustrated with an example. Take, for instance, the fictional insurance company Acme Insurance and Casualty. Acme is a nationwide company with subsidiaries in all 50 states. Because of stricter insurance regulations in some states, the subsidiary company in New York is not titled Acme Insurance and Casualty; rather, it is called Superior and Acme Insurance Company. They are separate legal entities, yet Acme Insurance and Casualty owns a substantial part of Superior and Acme Insurance Company.

Reinsurance: Reinsurance is the process by which insurance companies insure their investments; they are literally insuring again, just as the term translates. This concept fulfills a few different functions for the insurance company. First of all, it protects their assets. With reinsurance, a portion of the premiums collected by the insurance company would be used as a premium for insurance through a different company. This will help absorb large losses that an insurance company might face.

Look at one possible scenario where this may occur. Suppose that Bob, a client of Acme Insurance and Casualty, wishes to buy a $1-million term life insurance policy and invest $250,000 into a variable annuity. The $250,000 is paid for with a single premium, and the first premium of $2,000 for the $1 million is also paid at the time of signing the contracts. Both contracts go through the underwriting process and are approved. Nine more months of premiums go by so that now the insured has paid a grand total of $20,000 into the life insurance policy. Suddenly, Bob has a heart attack and passes away.

This is where things get complicated. During that ten-month period, the economy took a turn for the worse and the $250,000 has dropped drastically to become $200,000. When Bob signed his contract, he opted for a guarantee that would allow him to receive at least the full $250,000 in distributions, even if the annuity was not currently worth that much. Because Bob has given the insurance company $270,000, he is completely up to date with his investments, and as such, his heirs are eligible to receive the full amount. The heirs, however, choose to receive his inheritance from Acme as one lump sum. In other words, the insurance company now owes Bob's family $1,250,000.

In short, the insurance company only has $220,000 of the money available for Bob. Mortality pooling will help alleviate the cost here, but this is a hit of more than $1 million. Reinsurance would step in and cover the remainder of the loss. This is possible for the same reason creditors and banks can take out life insurance on their clients: They have an insurable interest in their clients. So, by purchasing their own life insurance on their clients through a separate company, the creditors would minimize their out-of-pocket expenses when their clients pass away.

Where Annuities Fit in
Your Portfolio

Some portfolios will have all of the investment products previously mentioned working simultaneously to earn you money. Even in this case, an annuity may still be a valuable part of your investment money and time. The closer you get to retirement, the more you want a predictable, reliable source of income. Cashing out the higher-risk investments that no longer make sense to retirees is, in most cases, a valuable reallocation of your money. This would include ETFs and stocks. In some cases, money market accounts should be dropped because the need to have a large available savings may not be necessary once you have a steady stream of income set up through an annuity.

If you have the funds available, you may still want to dabble in high-risk investments. In times of a good economy, this will greatly increase the amount of money you have to live off. But, your annuity, especially if you have a fixed annuity, will provide for you regardless of the current market conditions. Consult with a financial professional before making any major decisions or reallocations.

Chapter 2

Making Annuities Work for You

Annuities are a worthwhile investment for most retirees. If a 50-year-old is worried about saving money because he or she worries about longevity, starting to contribute a small portion of his or her income each month into an annuity will pay off. By the time investors are ready to retire, those small contributions will have added up. On top of this, he or she will have that money guaranteed — if he or she wishes — for the rest of his or her life. There are many different types of annuities out there — you simply need to pick the annuities and features that work best for you.

Paying for an Annuity

Annuities can be paid for in a certain number of ways. They can be funded by savings from accounts that are taxed quarterly or yearly, such as a money market account, savings account, or stock and bond holdings, meaning the stocks and bonds owned by the investor. Annuities can be bought with the earnings of tax-deferred accounts, such as IRAs or 401(k) plans. They can also be bought with an exchange of one annuity for another. If you have an annuity, because of Section 1035 of the Internal Revenue Code, you can transfer the money between annuities, regardless of the type, tax-free. This can be utilized to investors' advantage if the current annuity does not perform well. By filling out the exchange form specific to the state they are located in, they have the option, but not the obligation, to transfer their money from an underperforming annuity to a better one.

Lastly, annuities can be purchased with a sudden windfall of money, such as an inheritance left by a loved one who has passed away. No matter where your money comes from, however, there is probably an annuity that will fit your needs. This chapter is designed to show you what those needs are and how best to fulfill them.

In contrast to paying for an annuity is the concept of **self-insuring**. Self-insuring takes place when an individual stores enough cash in savings, checking, or other accounts so he or she may meet the demands associated with retirement. According to financial author Kerry Pechter, self-insuring may require up to 40 percent more money than purchasing an annuity. This is mainly because of the fact that not everyone passes away at the same time. Some people live much longer than their life expectancy; the longer someone lives, the more expenses they will have. In this case, paying out of pocket for your retirement comes at a hefty price.

You may find it more convenient to pay for flexible premium annuities with direct debits from your bank account. These automatic premium payments will give you one less thing to worry about. If you have a variable annuity, you will also need to decide how much money goes into each subaccount.

Identify Goals

The first step in choosing the investment product that is right for you is to identify your goals for the future. This should be your first order of business with any type of investment, regardless of what it is. Try jotting down the answers to the following questions:

1. Why are you purchasing this investment product?

2. What do you hope to accomplish with it?

3. Is the money you are investing expendable?

4. Are you willing to take a gamble with your financial future?

5. What would happen if you lost some or all of your investment?

6. What safeguards do you have in place in case of a loss of principal?

These questions may seem obvious, but they are vital to choosing the right product and features. Helping you know what to look for in an annuity and establishing the amount of risk you are willing to take with your investment, is by far the most important aspect of this book. The choices you will be confronted with when choosing an annuity, or any other investment product, can be overwhelming, and having a clear-cut vision of what you want to accomplish will guide you in the right direction. Speaking simplistically, if a secure investment that will guarantee a source of income for your retirement years is what you are looking for, an annuity is the right choice for you.

Determining risk levels

You will want to determine what kind of risk you are willing and able to take prior to selecting an annuity. Typically, the younger you are, the more aggressive you can afford to be with your money. The converse is also true — the older you are, the more conservative you should be. If you are on a fixed income, you will necessitate a more conservative investment than if you still have much earning capacity. There truly is an annuity for almost everyone, regardless of where you fall in the conservative and aggressive spectrum.

As a general rule, if you are looking for a conservative investment, you will look for something that returns around 3 to 5 percent, preferably in a guaranteed account. Aggressive investments can return upward of 18 percent, or even more, although they definitely do not perform this well year after year. It is important to take things like your age, your investment timeline, and your goals into account when determining your level of risk.

There is no exact way to determine what your risk level is; there are only approximations that can help you feel more comfortable with your investment. The questions in the last section should have given you a general idea of what type of risk you can assume. The following exercise will help you gain a more accurate look at your financial needs:

- Take the amount you have saved for retirement already, and add to it the amount you plan on saving in the future. This requires you to roughly approximate any raises in salary you may receive and to calculate how much you plan on saving each year. For example: If you make $40,000 per year and expect a raise of $1,000 per year, this is a total of $1,705,000 over the course of 30 years. Saving 10 percent of your income for these 30 years would equal $170,500.

- Next, calculate how many more years you plan on working. As of 2009 laws, nondisabled individuals can begin to receive social security benefits at age 62, with the full retirement age being 66. This means that if you elect to get your benefits at age 62, you will get a reduced amount, roughly 75 percent, of the full amount you would receive at age 66. Take social security benefits into account when determining your retirement age to help you determine how much you can save or how much money you will receive once you retire. For example: According to the Quick Calculator found at **www.ssa.gov**, A 65 year old retiring in 2010 who made $70,000 in his or her last year of work is entitled to roughly $1,707.00 per month. In addition to this amount, any other retirement savings from IRAs, pensions, or other investments would be added.

- Now, you need to calculate your expenses of daily living. Do you still have a mortgage? For how long will you be paying it off? What about groceries, car payments, leisure? Take everything you can think of into account. For example: A 65-year-old may have five to ten years left of payment on his or her mortgage. The hypothetical individual in this example owes $750 per month for ten more years. The person also has ten years left of car payments, at $300 per month. On top of this, the person pays $250 in utilities and $300 in groceries each month. This all adds up to $1,600, an amount covered by the individual's Social Security check of $1,707 per month. This means that the yearly expenses are $19,2000 (monthly expenses X 12) for this individual.

- This next step may seem morbid, but it is important. The average length of life in the United States for a female is 82, and a few years less for males, at age 75. Use this to get an accurate idea of your life expectancy and how long you will need to actually use your retirement funds you are about to invest in. How much money do you need during your retirement years? Use the following formula: (Yearly expenses X the amount of years you will be retired for). For example: The hypothetical individual may have a life expectancy of up to 85 years old. With $19,200 being spent per year, without inflation, this comes to a total of $384,000 that will be needed. Inflation, since the Great Depression, has risen about 3 percent per year, meaning that the value of a dollar drops by 3 percent each year. The amount you will need to maintain your style of living will then increase by this amount each year.

By way of contrast, the 35-year-old hypothetical individual earning $40,000 per year is planning on working until age 65. Working for another 30 years with an increase of about $1,000 per year gives the individual a total of $1,705,000. If the person can save 10 percent of his or her earnings, there is $170,500 that will have been put aside before earning any interest. Now, once the individual has reached age 65, they wish to buy an immediate annuity with that $170,500. If the individual has the money in a competitive IRA, it is more than realistic to round that number up to $350,000 thanks to the stock market's efficiency at keeping up with the rate of inflation. With the person's life expectancy at age 85, he or she will need a good rate of return to keep up with the expenses because self-insuring with the $350,000 is not enough. If the money was placed in an immediate annuity with a 6 percent rate of return, the person would receive $2,475.52 each month for 20 years. That comes to a total of $594,124.80. This does not take into account Social Security earnings or other investments. With Social Security at $1,707 per month, the individual can add another $409,680 to the nest egg for a total of $1,003,804.80 that he or she will receive over the course of the last 20 years of life, which works out to be $4,182.52 per month. Because this individual earned $70,000 in his or her last full year of working, he or she was earning $5,833.33 per month before retirement. If there was no other income coming in, the person would see a slight decline in his or her style of living at first, but this would quickly improve as he or she would pay off a mortgage and car loans rather quickly.

Once you have figured out how much you need to save using the previous suggestions, using the following questions will give you an idea of how you should go about saving that amount:

- How much expendable money can you set aside each month? Each year? Do you think this number will increase over time?

- Do you feel comfortable with an element of risk in your investments? How much can you risk?

- When the stock market declines, can you ride it out until stock prices rise once again? Or, do you feel more comfortable withdrawing money from the plan and holding it in low-risk cash accounts until a later date when market conditions are better?

These few questions should address your risk tolerance. If you are young, you will naturally have a higher tolerance for risk, while older individuals will have less tolerance. The young have a naturally higher risk tolerance because if they lose a portion of their investment, they will still have time to regain it. If your risk tolerance is on the low side, however, a fixed annuity may be more beneficial to you because you can guarantee the amount of savings you will have. If you have a higher degree of risk tolerance, you may consider a variable annuity, where your returns are not guaranteed but could be significantly more. These questions are only a starting point. Only you and your financial adviser can determine the exact point where you lie on the spectrum.

Diversify

You have probably heard the expression "do not put all your eggs in one basket." This quote gave birth to the investor's motto: "Diversify." Diversification can be a simple blend of high- and low-risk investments within one product, such as a variable annuity. It can also be a lower-risk element in a portfolio full of higher risk investments, such as a fixed annuity owned by a high-profile stock trader. Either way, annuities can be just the element of diversification your portfolio needs. As a product that offers many options, annuities themselves can be rich in diversity; for some people, an annuity will be the only investment they need to make. Annuities, as investments, are complex and multifunctional. This is also what makes them confusing. But, annuities offer many choices; making them a worthwhile investment. With so many choices to select from, it is more than likely you will find an annuity that meets your investing needs. As a safe and guaranteed alternative to the stock market, an annuity will add stability to any long-term investor's portfolio.

Variable annuities can act just like mutual funds when it comes to the allocation of funds. You have the option to choose which types of financial products your annuity consists of and what percentage of your funds you wish to have in each different product.

During the 2008-2009 recession, many investors saw a 40 to 50 percent loss within their investments. "We forgot the rule of diversification," said Paul Tran, president of Focal Point Financial Services, in an interview. "If we were really spread out correctly, we would've only lost 10 to 20 percent by some reports and could recoup losses easier than the real-life losses." By placing money correctly within retirement and other accounts, the short-term drops within the market can be minimized.

When to Invest

You can contribute capital to an annuity in two different ways: with a single premium or with multiple premiums. You may consider a single premium annuity if you have a sudden windfall of money, such as an inheritance, or if you are rolling over an older account. Rolling over accounts usually occurs with IRA and Roth IRA accounts because you must begin withdrawing from these accounts at a certain age. Oftentimes, investors are not ready to withdraw when they are required to at age 70½. Annuities work well in this respect because your money will continue to gain a competitive interest rate.

Multiple, also called flexible, premium annuities make sense for the average investor. This allows the investor to deposit capital into the annuity on a yearly or monthly basis as the money becomes available. In most contracts, there will be no set amount you have to contribute, giving you the maximum amount of flexibility.

Regardless of these options for annuities, some experts say the elderly should avoid investing their money in annuities. Even though there are always exceptions, an annuity is meant for long-term goals. If you wish to leave behind an inheritance, an annuity is certainly a capable tool, but you would have better results with your money in a life insurance policy, where the entire amount would avoid probate, as opposed to only the capital in an annuity.

But, there is a school of thought claiming that the sick and elderly should invest in annuities. The reasoning behind this is they will actually be purchasing their investment at a discount. **Impaired risk annuities**, as they are called, have larger distributions than regular annuities because the life expectancy of this group of people is shorter. This type of annuity is not widely sold because of the risk attached to it. Again, each case is different. It is up to the individual to decide what is best for him or her.

How much to invest

So, you have made the decision to invest in an annuity. Now, the question is how much money should you actually invest? Some experts argue that no more than 30 percent of your money should go into an annuity. This is because of the length of time associated with investing in annuities is ten or more years. Annuities are long-term investments and should be treated as such. In order for the tax-deferral benefits to be of any use, some experts say the money should be left alone for at least ten years, these experts argue. This is a long time to have your money locked up in an investment, and you will need money to live off in the meantime.

Others say you can invest up to 100 percent of your available money into annuities, providing you do so smartly. With **immediate income annuities**, you can provide an instant stream of income that will last for life. With this guarantee, why would anyone not want to invest all of their money? If you are in need of an income fast, this would be the perfect investment for you.

As you can see, it is not a cut-and-dry decision. Each individual needs to discover what method will work best for him or her. At different ages, different investment strategies will be more appropriate. This book is not meant to make the decision for you — this would be a very flawed objective — the purpose is to educate you as much as possible so you can make a more informed decision.

Inflation

Things cost more today than they did 30 years ago. Look at the price of gasoline, for example: A price once well below a dollar per gallon is now hovering around $3 per gallon. Although no one can predict the future, there are many indications that things will be more expensive in another 30 years. Historically, inflation has risen at an average of about 3 percent each year. Your money needs a way to combat this inflation; investing is the best way to do this. Annuities are a great investment tool because of their tax-deferred growth. They also offer a type of stability that other investments cannot provide. Although it is true that some annuities do not keep up with inflation, you can easily find those that will with a bit of research.

Retiring safely

You do not want your finances to cause you stress, especially once they are limited. An annuity will help you retire safely and securely and provide peace of mind like no other investment can. Fixed annuities are predictable and consistent investment products. The agent who sells you the annuity should be able to tell you approximately what kind of returns you will receive and for how long you should receive them. Some annuities even guarantee a source of income for the remainder of your life. Because they are tax-deferred, they will grow much more quickly in value than other products marketed for retirees, such as CDs. They will also earn money for you regardless of what the stock market does. Certainly, annuities will not earn you millions, but they will add value to your senior years by alleviating the worries that arise when you live on a fixed income by increasing your retirement funds.

Variable annuities, on the other hand, offer returns based on a portfolio of your choice. Because they are linked to a market index, there is a little bit of risk involved, and your principal is often not guaranteed. But, these annuities will normally outperform mutual funds of similar risk levels.

The company that sells you an annuity, regardless of what type you purchase, acts as a shield between you and your investment. This protects the investor from the daily dips and rises of the stock market. Rather than having a fluctuating product, the agency evens out the gains in order to provide investors with stable products.

Distributions

Distributions are the fun part of annuities. This is when you start to see your investment return to you. These can occur shortly after you sign your annuity contract or many years down the road depending on what type of annuity you purchase. Make sure you know what the stipulations are regarding your specific contract, as each company will have different rules built into their annuities.

The **surrender period** is the amount of time during which you are penalized for unauthorized distributions from your annuity. The industry average ranges from eight to ten years. Sometimes, surrender periods can be avoided if the investor decides to annuitize his or her contract early. After the surrender period is over and you decide you are ready to start your retirement and receive your money back, there are three main choices: withdrawal of a lump sum, systematic withdrawals, or annuitization. Each of these has advantages and disadvantages, outlined in the table below:

Lump sum withdrawal	This option gives the investor the most control over his or her money. Unfortunately, it also requires the investor to pay the appropriate taxes from the accumulated earnings back at one time.
Systematic withdrawals	With a systematic withdrawal, the money remaining in the annuity still earns interest, yet you have some control over it. This option does not guarantee income for life — the investor simply draws from his or her account until it is depleted.
Annuitization	Although this option gives you the least amount of control over your money, it can be the most beneficial, depending on your situation. If you elect to, you will be eligible to receive monthly distributions for the rest of your life, even if those distributions exceed the principal and interest you earn with your investment. This is accomplished through a phenomenon called risk pooling and will be discussed in Chapter 13.

Who Should Invest in an Annuity?

An annuity can meet almost anyone's needs, but there are a few qualifications you should consider before purchasing one. For instance, women have longer life expectancies than men. This makes them more likely to run out of income before they pass away, but an annuity can solve this problem by guaranteeing a life-long payment distribution.

People in higher tax brackets will also benefit from annuities because they delay the payment of taxes on a portion of their income. Earnings on annuities grow tax-deferred, meaning the amount of interest earned is only taxable once you begin to make withdrawals from your account. Once you retire and have a smaller income, you will fall into a lower tax bracket, making your annuity income much more manageable when it comes to taxation. You will no longer have your income from your place of employment to claim on tax forms; rather, you will only have your retirement funds to worry about.

If you do not have a defined retirement plan available to you at your workplace, an annuity is also a good idea because it will act as a supplement to Social Security benefits. With company **pensions** and 401(k) matching disappearing, the population with a clear-cut retirement program is quickly vanishing. Many companies, in an attempt to cut costs, have eliminated these programs. Social Security is a prime example of a pension. For the first time in more than 30 years, 2010 will not see an increase in Social Security benefits to retirees. Even the government is attempting to cut back on their costs regarding retirement. Because of this, it is even more important that individuals are prepared for their retirement.

Middle-class individuals are also great candidates for annuities. This includes the majority of Americans. Some analysts argue that for the most part, the upper class is self-insured and would probably take a pay cut by investing in annuities. The argument goes that they will most likely never run out of money, regardless of how long they live; and because of this, their money would go further in a life insurance policy because the entire amount would pass on tax-free to a beneficiary to take care of final expenses. Furthermore, because life insurance has a high degree of **arbitrage**, it will be more beneficial. With only a little money put into a life insurance policy, large gains can be realized for their heirs. For example, assume an individual is approved for a $500,000 policy for $50 a month, and upon receipt of the first $50 premium to the insurance company, the individual passes away. For only that $50, the insured's heirs will receive the whole $500,000. This does not mean, however, that the wealthy should completely rule out annuities. Everyone is vulnerable when market conditions are volatile. An annuity may provide the extra layer of protection investors look for.

Annuities are also a great tax shelter for the wealthy. Because the wealthiest Americans pay such a high percentage of taxes on their income, annuities can scale back on the amount they pay each year, paying for their earnings when they retire at a lower tax rate instead. If an individual has a portfolio of mutual funds, he or she must pay taxes each year for the earnings from that mutual fund. If the investor makes $80,000 per year at his or her place of employment and $10,000 with his or her mutual funds, he or she will be in the 28 percent tax bracket for 2009 because he or she will be earning more than $82,250 during the calendar year. The same individual would be in the 25 percent bracket, and thus pay a significantly lower amount in taxes if his or her money was in a tax-deferred annuity because this investor would still be in the 25 percent bracket because his or her income is less than $82,250 for the year.

Pessimists are also good candidates for annuities. People who believe the stock market will perform poorly should buy fixed annuities because they will turn a profit regardless of how the stock market performs. Even the biggest pessimist cannot frown when he or she receives income while so many others lose money during a downward cycle in the economy. There are some experts who claim that annuities are not worthwhile investments if you have a below-average life expectancy, but this is not always the case. Even if you do not believe you will live past age 65, an annuity can benefit you for the few years you have it by relieving the stress of living on a fixed income. It is also a way to avoid probate for your heirs — something that leaving your money in a savings or money market account will not accomplish. The need for annuities in this case might not be as strong, but it does not mean you should completely avoid them. Besides, you never know — you might live longer than you expect to. Having a reliable source of income will be extremely important in this case.

Focal Point Financial Services President Paul Tran said that the people who benefit the most from owning annuities are those who are wealthy. This is because much of their wealth is taken away by estate taxes and the probate process. "These families want to take care of their loved ones, donate their success to charities and foundations, and they can't do that to their fullest potential with the tax implications of a poorly planned estate strategy," Tran said.

Evaluating the Worth of an Annuity

Annuities add value to an investor's life in a few different ways. The first has to do with insurance. Annuities are an insurance product for a reason — they protect investors from running out of money when they live longer than expected. When compared to self-insuring, those without annuities to rely on spend 30 to 40 percent more during their retirement years. Annuities provide this type of savings because they grow tax-deferred, something that traditional savings approaches cannot claim.

Another reason why annuities provide worth is because they serve as a savings tool. Compared to a systematic withdrawal strategy, annuities are much easier. It has been ingrained into retirees to follow a **three-tier system** of savings: cash accounts that are easily accessible, bonds that provide steady and stable returns, and higher risk stock investments. Annuities, however, reduce the amount of work needed. Instead of keeping money in cash accounts, government bonds, and stocks, annuities not only save the investor money, but they also save on the amount of money management work necessary to fund a retirement.

Traditional investment advice claims that money needed throughout the course of the next year should be kept in cash accounts, such as money market accounts. This gives free or cheap access to savings while still earning a minimal rate of return. General purchasing and emergency money is thus kept easily on hand. Money needed in the near future should be kept in government or blue-chip corporate bonds, where it will earn a bit more interest, yet will mature and become available when the time comes.

Finally, money that will not be needed for quite some time is kept in the stock market where it has the potential to earn a higher interest rate and keep up with inflation.

This picture seems pretty thorough, but it does have some flaws. For one, it assumes that every retiree will actively manage his or her own money. Only the savviest of investors can do this successfully. It is a labor-intensive process that requires a good deal of expertise and time. Most retirees are not comfortable with taking on this responsibility.

Annuities, on the other hand, can ease this process. By providing a high rate of return and income for life, all three of the traditional approaches' components are covered in one investment. This saves time, money, and stress, allowing retirees to focus on something other than their finances. Annuities provide a peace of mind like no other investment.

General advantages of annuities

Tax-deferred growth is one of the biggest advantages of an annuity. You will not pay taxes on your annuity until you start withdrawing growth or interest from it. This means that not only is your principal earning interest but also that the amount that would be subtracted because of taxation earns interest. You are also free from taxes in the event that you wish to exchange your annuity for a more beneficial one.

When compared to other retirement products, annuities may seem lacking at first. In most cases, there is no employer matching, and they involve post-tax dollars, making them nondeductible on your income tax form. But, there is no limit to what you can contribute into an annuity, and there is no limit as to how many annuities you may own. This is something no other product can claim and another obvious advantage of annuities. A well-planned set of annuities can make your retirement years the most fruitful years of your life.

General disadvantages of annuities

There is a risk with annuities that should be addressed upfront — there are fees and penalties for withdrawing money prior to the **maturity date**. You should pay special attention to how your annuity will be annuitized because once this period begins, it cannot be altered. Annuities are a contract between you and the financial services group you decide to go with. It is impossible to access all of your money, even in the case of an emergency, without penalties once the annuitization occurs. These penalties differ from company to company and depend on how long you have had the annuity. As a rule, insurance companies will charge you around 10 percent of your investment if you do decide you need your money more quickly.

Although annuities are renowned for their tax advantages, there are some disadvantages that must be discussed. Besides a few exceptions, such as death or total disablement, withdrawals prior to age 59½ are charged 10 percent in taxes by the IRS. There are also fees and penalties enforced by insurance companies that sell annuities that help keep your money with them for longer periods. These penalties can be avoided if you are of retirement age simply by choosing to annuitize your investment a bit early.

Some insurance companies also charge a mortality fee. This fee is not taken out of your primary investment, but rather skimmed away from the percentage you would earn. The money diverted in this manner is used to pay guaranteed death benefits.

Another common fee is the annual maintenance fee. Some companies will charge up to $50, while others waive this fee completely.

Surrendering an annuity will make any gains taxable as income for the tax year the surrender is processed during. Another disadvantage is the fact that if the death benefit is used, the beneficiary is taxed on the entirety of the earnings in the distribution. In order to ease this burden, beneficiaries are allowed to spread distributions over the course of five years.

These disadvantages should not deter you from investing in an annuity. Annuities are designed to aid in retirement planning. As long as you pay attention to, and agree with, the method in which your investment will be returned to you, there is nothing to worry about.

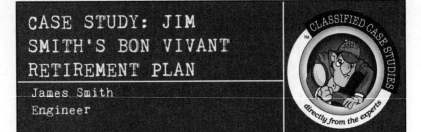

James Smith is an engineer with a global automotive supplier in upstate New York. After working at various positions within his industry for 25 years, his current focus is to manage enterprise-wide reductions in cost. Smith focuses mainly on his company's operations in Brazil and China, giving him a truly global outlook on his life. Smith began saving for retirement early in his career. Later, he learned he was to receive an inheritance. After the money sat in a money market fund for a while gaining minimal amounts of interest, Smith decided he needed something more from his money.

Life is an adventure for Smith and a blessing. While he planned to reach the 30-year mark of being in his industry, he actively prepared for his retirement years. Like many new retirees, he wished to relocate to a warmer climate and use his time to volunteer for the less fortunate. Travel is another wish of Smith's. A history enthusiast, he plans on visiting historical Gettysburg and Mount Rushmore. His annuities will help make these wishes viable. Now, instead of worrying about money, the insurance company does the work and gives him much more in way of returns than his money market account did. Peace of mind for Smith does not come at a cost; it is paying him.

Smith owns two annuity contracts: one fixed and one variable. The fixed annuity was purchased first for $50,000 and has a 4.25 percent return for the first three years. After this period elapses, the rate is guaranteed not to fall less than 3 percent.

When deciding what type of annuities to invest in, Smith turned to his main passion: chess. A student of the game for many years, Smith truly knows the necessity of planning ahead. This is why he bought a variable annuity for $20,000 in order to keep his money in a more competitive account. This annuity is spread out over a number of mutual funds and is rebalanced automatically on a quarterly basis so his money stays where he needs it.

This mixture of funds — in fixed and variable form — allows for safety of his principal amount, while also presenting an opportunity for maximizing his gains. All the while, Smith enjoys a tax-deferred profit.

By choosing to invest his money with New York Life, Smith has enjoyed a few accoutrements. The first of these is he met with an agent face to face. New York Life is a trusted and fiscally solid company, and the agent Smith met with reflected this. Smith has met with the same agent a few times over the course of his contract.

Like any good chess player, Smith has prepared himself for retirement in other areas as well. With a fully vested 401(k), a Roth IRA, and the promise of his company pension and social security, Smith has his positions covered, and more importantly, is satisfied with his situation.

Things to Consider When Purchasing an Annuity

- Does this annuity relieve the amount of stress I will face?

- Will investing my money in an annuity lower the amount of money I pay in income taxes?

- Does this annuity coincide with the amount of risk I am willing to face?

The Complete Guide to Investing in Annuities

Chapter 3

Annuity Misconceptions

There are two major kinds of annuities — fixed and variable — and a plethora of different features within them, including equity-indexed annuities. This chapter is meant to clearly define what annuities are and what they are not, while addressing common questions and misconceptions As you will see, annuities have a broad range of attributes, but there are a few key factors that all annuities share.

What is an Annuity?

Annuities are insurance products that act as investments. There are dozens of variations of annuities, but all of them share some common characteristics.

Tax Deferral: All annuities grow tax-deferred, meaning they are not taxable until you start to receive money from them. Profits from annuities are taxed on a last-in, first-out basis, meaning you pay the taxes on your annuity when you first start to withdraw from it because you will be technically withdrawing the earnings from your annuity first. The benefit of this is that as you age, you will pay less and less in taxes from your annuity.

Minimum Distribution Age: According to IRS laws, you cannot start receiving distributions from an annuity penalty-free until you have reached age 59½. There are exceptions to this rule, however, such as death and complete and permanent disablement. In these cases, the annuitant or the annuitant's beneficiary, can receive distributions early. This is meant to encourage the use of the money invested solely for retirement.

Payout Options: There are various manners in which you can choose to receive distributions once you annuitize your investment. The most popular of these includes an investment you cannot outlive. The straight life option will provide an annuitant with a life-long stream of income, no matter how long the annuitant lives. Once you do annuitize the contract, you can choose when and how you receive distributions.

Death Benefit: Annuities bypass probate and go directly to a beneficiary without the messy affairs of distributing an estate. You will as a survivor, in most cases, be asked to provide a copy of the death certificate in the event you are named a beneficiary in a loved one's annuity.

When annuity funds are distributed after an annuitant's death, the principal amount in a nonqualified annuity is received tax-free, with only the interest being taxable. If considered a qualified plan, taxes are paid on the entire amount received. Depending on the contract, death benefits are received in one lump sum or over the course of several payments. Some companies will even allow you to continue the accumulation period if the heir does not wish to collect the money right away.

The one exception to the death benefit is an annuity with a straight life option. These annuities will only pay out to a living annuitant. Although this seems like a poor idea, the straight life option does afford the annuitant with the highest amount of distributions out of all other options.

Free Look Period: All annuities have a free look period, but the amount of time for these varies from state to state. The most common free look periods are between ten and 30 days, although some companies may elect to have longer periods. This period is common for all insurance products and refers to the time between when you receive the final policy, either by mail or agent delivery, and when you can cancel the policy without incurring a penalty. This is especially beneficial to those coerced into signing a contract by a high-pressure salesman.

Stability: Annuities offer stability regardless of market conditions. Fixed annuities and even most variable annuities have guarantees that no other product can match. By reducing risk, an annuity could be the cornerstone of your investment portfolio.

Annuities are growing in popularity as well. As the baby boomer generation nears retirement, annuities are soaring in popularity. They offer lifetime benefits that no other investment product can match. You can count on these products becoming even more investor-friendly as the growing needs of the boomers are taken into account. And, with pensions being reduced by employers, something needs to be done to protect financial futures.

What an Annuity is Not

Annuities are not get-rich-quick investments, and thus are not meant as short-term investments. They are designed for an investor's retirement years, and federal tax laws have been constructed to reinforce this. Because you cannot, in most cases, withdraw money without penalty from an annuity prior to age 59½, annuities have a safeguard built into them so they will encourage investors to prepare for retirement.

Good to Know:

Mutual funds and annuities have a few things in common. For one, they both have wonderful track records as far as returns go. You can also customize your investment with either mutual funds or annuities to get the most return, and they both offer systematic withdrawal options for when you need your money. In most cases, you can start either investment with just a few hundred dollars.

There are some major differences between annuities and mutual funds. For example, most mutual funds will charge the investor some sort of commission fee. This can be as little as 1 percent of your total investment, but it is still money you will lose. With fixed annuities, the agent who sells you your investment will still get paid for the sale, but you will not be responsible for this payment. The entirety of what you invest goes to work for you. The agent selling you the annuity is simply rewarded with money from the insurance company. Variable annuities, however, will charge fees similar to those of mutual funds.

Another difference is taxation. With a mutual fund, you are charged taxes in three instances: yearly gains, gains when the fund manager sells or receives profits from shares, and gains realized when you sell off portions of your fund. Taxes are taken out of annuities only once you start withdrawals.

Safety is another key point that differs between a mutual fund and an annuity. By law, a mutual fund cannot give you a guarantee. Annuities can make guarantees because they are classified as insurance products. Except in very rare cases, annuities follow through on this guarantee, whereas many people have lost money while investing in mutual funds. This leads to a last difference: performance. The top-performing variable annuities normally outperform top mutual funds. There are always exceptions, but variable annuities tend to outperform their mutual fund counterparts.

Common Annuity Misconceptions

The following questions and statements are misconceptions that people often associate with both the purchasing and owning of annuities. These misconceptions are addressed and corrected so you can understand the truth behind annuities and make a clear decision about which type of annuity — if any — is right for you.

"I heard that I should only invest with big name companies."

Although it is true that most big name companies have been around for a long time, you should base your decision more on the interest rate being offered with past and present annuities. You would recognize a big name company as one that spends a lot of money on television and other media advertising. These include Prudential, American Family Life Assurance Company of Columbia (Aflac), and State Farm Insurance. You should also take time to research a particular company's fiscal rating through independent ratings agencies, such as A.M. Best (**www. ambest.com**). Smaller companies, such as MassMutual® (**www.massmutal.com/**) or Bankers Life and Casualty (**www.bankers.com**), are sometimes able to offer higher rates than the bigger companies, and their independently gauged strength ratings may be just as good or better.

"I do not need an annuity because I already have life insurance."

Annuities may be insurance products, but they do not replace the necessity of life insurance. The opposite is also true. Owning life insurance does not replace the need for an annuity. Even though they may both have tax-free death benefits, annuities are designed to aid in your retirement years by guaranteeing you a source of income. Life insurance is designed to cover final expenses, such as funerals, debts, and gifts for heirs. There is some overlap in these products, but they are not completely interchangeable. In fact, annuities are a type of insurance you will want to actually use; they are used to provide an income for you long into your retirement years.

"If I die, my beneficiaries will receive nothing."

This is a possibility with some types of annuities but only if you want it to be. These annuities, known as straight life annuities, also offer the highest returns while you are living but nothing to your heirs when you pass away. Ultimately, this is your choice: Do you want to receive the maximum benefits while living or preserve a portion of your assets for your final expenses and heirs? This is something you will definitely want to discuss with your agent so you make the best choice for you and your family.

"An annuity will affect how much I receive in Social Security."

This is not true. Your Social Security benefits are determined by the amount of money you made in your career during your top 35 working years. These 35 years are averaged together, and your monthly Social Security benefit is determined from that number. Because annuities are accessed later in life and are considered a supplemental income, they will not affect the amount you receive as your monthly Social Security benefit.

"Annuities do not perform well in bad markets."

This is only partly true. A fixed annuity will guarantee you a small, yet reliable return, even when the stock market is going through a rough time. Remember: Something is better than nothing. While variable annuities might report losses quarter after quarter, your fixed annuity will continue to grow. And, when the market corrects itself, you can always transfer your account to a variable annuity.

Fixed annuities are a predictable alternative to the stock market. If you are a bear when it comes to the market, this type of annuity may suit your needs. Annuities can make money in any market thanks to the guarantees provided by insurance companies. Because these companies invest mainly in bonds, their income remains steady even during the worst market times.

"Annuities do not take inflation into account."

Many people are worried that the nation's inflation rate will increase more drastically than their investment, leaving them with less buying power than what they started out with. This is only partially true; it must be admitted that some annuities are not competitive when inflation is taken into account. But, these products are in the minority. This is why you must shop around. With a little bit of research, it is possible to find annuities that will not only keep up with inflation but will also surpass it. Education on what rates are available to consumers is definitely a mandatory part of annuity shopping.

Variable annuities were created to address the issue of inflation. Even some fixed annuities take this into account. If combating inflation is important to you, as it should be with any long-term investment you make, shop around so you find the companies that best handle this problem.

In order to see how inflation may affect your investment, consider the following example: According to **http://data. bls.gov/cgi-bin/cpicalc.pl**, $100 dollars in 1980 is equal to $261.76 in 2009. This is roughly 3 percent interest per year over the 29-year period. If combating inflation is important to you, you will want to find an annuity that has guarantees more than the 3 percent threshold. This means you may need to shop around in order to find the annuity that best meets your needs. Agents may be well versed in their own products, but it is ultimately your responsibility to determine which product is best.

"I already have an IRA. Do I need an additional annuity?"

The answer to this question should be determined by the goals you have already established. Is your 401(k) or IRA large enough to meet your wants and needs during retirement? Do you want to maintain your standard of living, or will you be scaling back? What if you live longer than expected? An additional annuity can also prevent you from outliving your money, something your IRA probably will not do.

With traditional IRAs, withdrawals must begin at age 70½, or you will face a tax penalty of up to 50 percent of the amount you are required to withdraw. With life expectancy on the rise, age 70½ is still considered young. According to World Development Indicators, the average lifespan of an American between 1960 and 2007 has risen from 70 to 78 years. In this light, it should be noted that it is possible to roll over IRAs into commercial annuities in order to avoid withdrawing money too early. In short, an annuity is still a valuable investment even if you have an IRA as long as you do not invest short-term money into the annuity.

"I only need an annuity if I have maxed out my yearly IRA contribution."

If you are able to maximize your contributions to an IRA, you should. The current yearly contribution amount is $5,000 per investor or $6,000 if you are older than 50.

IRAs have a major benefit that annuities do not have: an income tax deduction feature. If you contribute the maximum legal amount into an IRA, when you fill out your tax papers, you can deduct this amount from your income so it is virtually a pre-tax contribution. Not all annuities will allow this. But, that does not mean you should only contribute to an IRA. Examining rates of return between the two types of investments will help you decide which one works best for you. There is no limit to the amount you can contribute to an annuity over the course of a year, making them a great place to store cash. IRAs cannot boast this fact.

Another factor in choosing an annuity over an IRA is that some annuities offer life-long payouts regardless of how long you live, something IRAs cannot offer. Because of the existence of subtypes of annuities, such as advanced life deferred annuities and straight life annuities, the risk of longevity is addressed, whereas noninsurance products like IRAs fail to do so. It is a very real possibility that an investor can outlive his or her IRAs distributions.

"Insurance agents are not any good at financial planning."

Your insurance agent might not have a CFP (Certified Financial Planning degree), but ask yourself this question: Is your financial planner a good salesman? Odds are, the answer to this question is yes. With commission charges and maintenance fees, your financial planner makes a lot of money off you. Is the money market account he recommends in your best interest, or his? Annuities can only be sold by people with life insurance licenses, something many financial planners lack and, therefore, will not recommend because they will not make any money off an annuity. It is important for you to determine if your financial planner has your best interests in mind.

The same applies to insurance agents. They are first and foremost salespeople. Most insurance agents will only be paid if they produce. Although the vast majority of insurance agents act ethically, it should be noted that some will suggest products that are in their best interest and not yours. Make sure the annuity you are looking at will benefit you more than it will benefit the person you are purchasing it from.

"Mutual funds have lower costs and are not taxed as highly."

The costs associated with mutual funds are normally perceived to be lower than those applied to variable annuities. This is simply not accurate. True, some annuities have higher costs than similar mutual funds, but this is not a trend that is indicative of each and every product.

When it comes to capital gains taxes, there are mixed perceptions as well. While the capital gains tax was at 15 percent in early 2010 and most individuals were taxed at a higher rate for income taxes, there is wiggle room within the tax laws. The aptly name "turnover ratio" assigns a percentage number to the amount of sales that took place within a mutual fund's holdings. The higher the turnover ratio, the more transactions that are taking place, and the more likely you will be to see high commissions. It also makes you more likely to see a higher capital gains tax bill because you will be charged capital gains taxes for each position your mutual fund broker closes so you will be hit twice as hard. If you still want to go with a mutual fund, make sure it has a low turnover ratio.

Common Annuity Mistakes

There are a few mistakes commonly made when purchasing annuities. The first is investing too much in them. Although this book asserts that almost everyone should have an annuity, it does not mean you should have *only* an annuity. You should not invest money you will need to survive from day to day. Annuities are long-term investments and should be treated as such. This means you should stash emergency cash in some other type of investment, such as a money market account, which will be readily accessible should you need it.

Another mistake often made is withdrawing too much during the annuitization period. You should know exactly how much money you need to survive when you plot out your annuitization structure. Forming a budget once you are on a fixed income is an important part of anyone's financial health. You should also factor in needs like entertainment and luxury money. But, you do not need to withdraw more than that. Withdrawing too much is a quick way to outlive your income.

You may have purchased a fixed annuity that is no longer competitive. This may be the case because newer fixed annuities may offer higher rates, or your current annuity may no longer be able to keep up with the rate of inflation. If you are still in the accumulation phase, it might be in your best interest to exchange your investment for a more competitive annuity. Each month, insurance companies will update their rates to coincide with how their holdings perform. The fixed annuity you purchased a few months ago might earn less than current annuities from the same company if market conditions drastically approve. You may even want to consider a variable annuity because they take stock market increases into account, something that has historically been rising since the Great Depression ended.

The biggest mistake you could make, however, is not doing your homework. The options are almost unlimited regarding your choices for annuities and the features of the annuity you choose. By not shopping around, you severely limit yourself and your future source of income. Plenty of websites compare insurance products available in your state, including annuities. Do not make this mistake — it is often the first in a series of mistakes when it comes to choosing an annuity.

Annuities, as you have seen, are complex, and there are many different types to choose from. The following chapters will break down each type of annuity to help you decide which one is the right investment for you.

There are two major subtypes of annuities: **qualified** and **nonqualified**. This simply refers to the tax status of the money invested. Qualified annuities are purchased with pre-tax dollars. These normally take form as an IRA or a Roth IRA. There are limits to how much you can contribute each year to these types of qualified annuities. Another variation of qualified annuities can be found in the not-for-profit sector under the guise of 403(b) plans.

Nonqualified annuities account for the majority of commercial annuities. These are purchased with post-tax dollars, grow tax-deferred, and, upon withdrawal, are taxed on a last-in, first-out basis. Because the principal amount is comprised of post-tax dollars, only the earnings are taxed. There is no limit to how much you may invest per year in a nonqualified account.

Within these two subtypes, annuities can be classified under three major headings: fixed annuities, variable annuities, and equity-indexed annuities that are connected to a stock market index.

Key Points to Remember When Shopping for Annuities

- Shopping for an annuity is a complex process. You need to take many factors into account when making a decision.

- Inflation can cause havoc upon an outdated annuity. Historically, inflation has risen at about 3 percent each year. If your annuity is making less than 3 percent, you should consider finding a new annuity.

Chapter 4

Fixed Annuities

Fixed annuities are just what they sound like: an annuity with a fixed minimum interest rate of return. They are the most basic and consistent annuities available. In fact, they are often compared to Certificates of Deposit because of the locked in rate of return and the time commitment that is made. Money put into these accounts earns interest at a rate stipulated in the contract and will not fall below the guaranteed minimum rate, which is where the "fixed" comes from. But, like any investment, there are advantages and disadvantages to these annuities.

Basic Facts

A fixed annuity is a contract that stipulates a minimum interest rate that your investment will never fall below. Some fixed annuities will offer rates much higher than the guaranteed minimum. Others will offer high rates for the first year as a bonus for signing up and then fall back to the minimum guaranteed rate. Again, it is up to you to research and shop around to determine which type of fixed annuity is right for you. There are literally hundreds of different fixed annuities, making your odds of finding one that meets your needs very good.

Premiums collected for fixed annuities are placed in the insurance company's general account, meaning each investor's premiums are lumped together in the same fund. The money is then mostly invested in different types of bonds. This can further be divided into separate portfolios for ease of supervision, but all money is kept together, making management much easier.

The major downfall of the general account is that if the company you invest in goes bankrupt, the general account is subject to the claims of creditors. This rarely occurs because each company must prove its solvency to the state insurance department. If a bankruptcy were to occur, a fiscally healthy insurance company would be given control of the accounts. This means that if the company you were to invest with should go bankrupt, your annuity funds would be taken over by a different, more stable company.

Types of fixed annuities

Single Year: With this type of annuity, the insurance company gives the investor a fixed rate that is guaranteed for one year. At the end of the year, the insurance company has the option of raising or lowering the rate your annuity is earning; this is called the **renewal rate**. It is important that you are aware of what historical renewal rates have been if you choose this type of annuity. In most cases, the renewal rate will decline, especially if the overall market has performed poorly.

It is in the annuitant's best interest to have higher rates for renewal because that means they will earn more interest on his or her investment. Realistically, it is not feasible to expect higher rates each year, but it does pay off to research how well the company's annuities have performed historically. This will give you a better idea of what you can expect in good, as well as weak, market times.

Multiple Years: This type of annuity will have a guaranteed rate for a predetermined number of years. These annuities are much more predictable than single year annuities because they have a set interest rate that the investor will always be rewarded with; they can never be lowered.

When the period specified in a multiple year guaranteed contract expires, there are a few options. The money can be withdrawn and used, or it can be left in the annuity and earn interest at the rate the insurance company offers for an additional year. Another option is to roll the annuity over into a new annuity. If you are happy with the interest rates your current company offers, you can elect to stay with the same company. Value shopping with other companies is also an option if you think you can get better returns elsewhere.

Floating Rates: Some annuities offer contracts with an interest rate that varies from month to month. These are largely determined by the financial status of the insurance company. A good month will reward the investor, but if the company has a bad fiscal month, you can be sure that rates will lower. In return for the uncertainty that these contracts have, they will sometimes offer a window of **penalty-free withdrawals** at some point during the year.

Stability

Fixed annuities are great for people who need a budget. You will always know at any given time the minimum your investment returns. When it comes time to annuitize your contract, you can count on steady and consistent distributions. A fixed annuity is perfect for people on fixed incomes because of this. If Social Security is your only source of income, yet you have savings, consider an immediate fixed annuity in order to maximize the return on your savings while not compromising the principal in higher-risk investments, such as a mutual fund.

There is no fixed annuity that will work for everyone. Each is a different and unique product based upon the company's contract. There are some that do offer flexibility with the amount of time you must have your money in them. If you think the interest rates will go up in the future, it might be in your best interest to opt for a shorter contract.

Interest rates

Fixed annuities offer guaranteed interest rates that will change periodically. Your **minimum interest rate**, however, will be locked in when your contract is processed. Your annuity will never fall below this percentage. These are great investments because they offer stability and predictability because you will be notified what the current interest rate is of your annuity and will be able to plan accordingly. There are a few different interest rates that investors should be aware of.

Initial Interest Rate: As the name suggests, this is the interest rate your annuity will earn when first opened. Depending on the company, this interest rate will be in effect for anywhere from a few months to a few years. Bonus rates are included in this category. Be careful when dealing with bonus rates — the higher the rate, the longer your surrender period might be. The surrender period is the amount of time between the beginning of the contract and when you can withdraw money penalty-free. This factor may delay your access to your money for several years. It may also be a mask for an inferior product, as a large bonus is only so effective if the product has an extremely low interest rate in subsequent years.

Current Interest Rate: This is the rate that the annuity currently credits to your account. Current interest rates do change depending on the market and the company's financial standing. It may be the minimum, or if the company is doing well financially, it may be higher than the guaranteed minimum.

Minimum Guaranteed Interest Rate: The interest credited to your account will never fall below this mark. This rate will be established in the contract and should be shared with you by the agent prior to signing any documents.

Multiple Interest Rates: Some annuities may offer different interest rates with each premium you pay. It is important to fully understand your contract so you know what interest rate you are receiving and when. This term is sometimes known as a floating rate.

Renewal Rates: The renewal rate refers to the rate given to your investment after the first year. You may have a bonus rate that disappears after the first year. The insurance company you choose may not know what the renewal rate will be after your first year is over, but make sure to find out what they are paying on older contracts. This will give you a basic idea of what they will pay out on yours if the economy does not change drastically.

In addition to the various interest rates, you should be aware that your actual initial interest rate may change between the time you sign the contract and when the insurance company actually processes your money. With some companies, interest rates vary from month to month. You may be expecting a 6 percent initial rate, and actually get a 5.8 percent rate if you sign your contract near the end of the month, and the rate drops the following month. This will happen because of the inevitable delay that paperwork entails. These situations do arise, but unless the company faces drastic problems, the variation will be minimal, as it is in the previous example. This situation is especially true if your contract involves an **exchange**. Exchanges take longer to process since the new company must contact your old annuity company.

A word regarding fees

At first glance, most fixed annuities do not seem to charge any fees. Your principal is guaranteed, as is the fixed rate offered by the insurance company. So, how do the agent and the company get compensated for selling you the annuity? The answer is in the rate of return the annuitant earns over the course of the contract. Fixed annuity rates are artificially lowered in order for the people involved in the selling and handling of the annuity to get paid. If the insurance company's actual profit in their general account and other holdings is 10 percent, then they may guarantee a rate of 3 percent on all fixed annuities. The 7 percent difference is where the insurance company makes their money.

Another necessity of fixed annuities is the surrender period. The surrender period is the length of time when the annuitant cannot access all of his or her money without incurring a penalty. By forcing the client to stay in the contract for upward of ten years, the insurance company has more than enough time to recover from any poor market times or outrageous bonus rates. Beware of long surrender periods, as they lock your money up unless you are willing to pay a fee. Surrender periods are yet another way the insurance company can make money off your investment.

Advantages of Fixed Annuities

Some of the advantages of fixed annuities have already been discussed. These annuities offer a minimum amount of return, even in the worst market conditions. The same is true for your principal amount — it is also guaranteed by the insurance company. Because of this, fixed annuities are great investments for people looking to map out exactly what they expect in return. You can safely count on fixed annuities to send you that monthly or yearly check you need.

In good market times, you can count on higher returns as well. These returns might not be as good as a variable annuity during the same market situation, but most companies will adjust your rate of return to reflect how well the company is doing. If your fixed annuity rate is guaranteed at 4 percent and the market is doing well, you may see rates as high as 6 or 7 percent on your annuity.

Fixed annuities are also great for people looking for an immediate source of income. Because there is no risk you will lose your principal and you are guaranteed a minimum interest rate, fixed annuities thrive as a source of income for retirees.

In a nutshell, fixed annuities are designed for the more conservative investors. This generally means that retirees and the elderly should steer toward this type of investment. Paul Tran of Focal Point Financial & Insurance Services observed that during poor market there is a huge increase in the sale of fixed and indexed annuities. This is because the rates guaranteed are far better than the loss potential investors would experience if their money was kept in the stock market.

Disadvantages of Fixed Annuities

The rate of return, which is normally considered an advantage, can also be seen as a disadvantage for the same reason: After the first year, you cannot be completely sure what your rate of return will be. No one, not even the best economists, can predict market conditions a year or two down the road. Your rate of return is guaranteed, but there is no way you can predict how much more than that rate your profits will actually be. True, you can bank on the minimum and consider the rest icing on the cake, but you cannot tell exactly how much higher the rate of return will actually be.

Inflation is another significant disadvantage. This is more of a factor after the annuitization period begins. If you begin collecting distributions from your annuity, your fixed rate becomes locked in. The longer you receive payouts, the less purchasing power that payout has because of inflation. However, if the rate of return you receive becomes too low during the accumulation period, you always have the option of transferring your money into a more competitive annuity, tax-free.

Another disadvantage of fixed annuities is that you give up control of your money. In other words, the insurance company decides how to allocate your funds. This may or may not be in the same manner you would choose. If you want simplicity in your investments though, this could be to your benefit for the same reason.

How to Tell if a Fixed Annuity is the Right Type of Annuity for Me

Are you on a fixed income? Do you wish you had a better return on your savings, yet you do not want to put your money in an investment that is not guaranteed? If you answered yes to both of these questions, a fixed annuity is perfect for you. You want to be able to plan exactly what money you have coming in, and what money you are spending. A fixed annuity will certainly help you plan your retirement more exactly.

This might not be the right investment for you if you are young and still have a steady income through your employer. Variable annuities, although most do not guarantee your principal, may be a better option because they are linked to a group of stocks or other investment vehicles of your choice. Over longer periods, these variable annuities historically outperform fixed annuities, and even most mutual funds. The potential for gains is greater in a variable annuity than in any other type of annuity. But, remember, because they are variable products, there is always the possibility of a decline in value. *See Chapter 5 for more details about this.*

The purchasing power of an annuitized fixed annuity declines as inflation progresses. As a trade-off, with most fixed annuities, you are guaranteed an income for life. Fixed annuities, therefore, address one of the many risks of aging: the fact that an individual may outlive his or her savings.

A fixed annuity will be especially helpful for married couples. With a fixed annuity, both spouses can be covered within the annuity contract. In the event that a spouse passes away, the survivor can still have the same income with the **joint and 100 percent survivor payment option**. Lesser percentages, such as joint and 50 percent survivor or joint and 25 percent survivor, can also be chosen if desired. The lesser the percentage given to a survivor, the higher the distribution will be to the annuitant while he or she is living.

Chapter 5

Variable Annuities

A variable annuity is an annuity connected to the performance of some other financial product; whether it be stocks, mutual funds, or bonds. Variable annuities differ greatly from fixed annuities because of this. The money you invest into this type of annuity is normally not guaranteed but has the potential to earn much more than a fixed annuity because your premiums are connected to a market of your choice. The funds are allocated according to the level of risk you are willing to take with your investment, each level corresponding to an appropriate subaccount. You will either be rewarded or you will lose money based on the risks you choose to take with your annuity.

Basic Facts

Variable annuities were created to solve the major problem of fixed annuities: protection against inflation. With fixed annuities, once the annuitization period begins, the distributions are locked in. You cannot increase what you get as a distribution. If and when inflation occurs, fixed annuities do not change their payouts. Over time, the purchasing power of a fixed annuity will become weaker because of this.

Variable annuities offer a degree of freedom that fixed annuities do not have. They also offer a flexibility that fixed annuities cannot provide. You have the option of changing your investment portfolio at a moment's notice as your wants and needs change. This is done through reallocation of assets into different risk classes. With a fixed annuity, there are no choices — the insurance company simply and completely manages your money.

Variable annuities are funded with flexible premiums rather than a one-time, lump-sum payment. This allows you to tailor your contributions to your needs at the time and even skip a payment if it is necessary.

There are still options that allow you to have inexhaustible benefits for life, even within the world of variable annuities. This would give you the highest monthly distribution checks. Other options similar to fixed annuities also exist, such as period or amount certain. The main difference is that you are held more responsible for your investment choices.

As far as internal asset allocation is concerned, variable annuities must create separate accounts. These accounts will have subaccounts the investor can choose to invest in at his or her own free will. The **subaccounts** are then invested in wherever their title suggests they be placed; aggressive subaccounts would be investing in small cap business stock, growth subaccounts in governmental bonds, and so on.

The purpose of the separate account is to protect the investors' money from creditors. It is a rare occurrence for an insurance company to go belly-up, but in the event that it does, the separate account protects the investors' capital. If the company you invest with does happen to go bankrupt, your balance, as calculated at the date of bankruptcy, would remain safe. Remember though, you may not retain all of your original principal because variable annuities oftentimes fluctuate up and down in their price.

Evaluating Your Risk Tolerance

If you are looking to an annuity for retirement purposes, odds are you are looking for reliable and consistent returns. Variable annuities do pose a bit of risk to your investment, but they are more lucrative than a mutual fund with a similar risk profile would be over the same period. In addition, variable annuities can provide a stream of income for the remainder of the annuitant's life, a benefit that mutual funds cannot claim.

Still, there are risks associated with variable annuities, and you should know what they are prior to purchasing one. Before you decide where you want your money to go, ask yourself the following questions:

How Will I Feel if I Lose Some of this Money? Variable annuities are still meant to be used as long-term investments, but stock market crashes do occur, and this may affect your investment. If you can stomach a loss, maybe a higher-risk annuity is your best option. If the thought of losing even a little makes you squeamish, you will want to navigate toward a more stable option. Crashes are inevitable, and it can take years to rebuild your wealth if they are severe. If you are not comfortable with this, select a fixed annuity.

How Much of this Money do I Actually Need? You may be one of the lucky few who has a lot more money than you actually need to live off. If this is the case, you will probably not mind losing some of it if the market sours. In this instance, you will want to get the most bang for your buck and invest in a more aggressive portfolio. You will still want a portion of your investment in a stable growth account, though. Remember, diversification is the key to consistently stable returns.

Why Do I Want a Variable Annuity? What has attracted you to a variable annuity in the first place? Is it the fact that in good years, your returns will be much higher than a fixed annuity? If this is the case, you will want at least a portion of your money in an aggressive subaccount. Maybe you were attracted to this type of annuity because of the ease and flexibility in premium options. Dollar cost averaging, as you will see, has the potential for great returns.

What are My Goals? This goes back to the goals you set forth earlier in this book. The goals you have will always be a work in progress, but writing them down will make you much more aware of what you actually want to accomplish in the here and now. If your goals are lofty and far in the future, a more aggressive plan may benefit you. If you simply want a plan to get you through the expenses of daily living, you will want a more stable investment.

Investment Choices

You have many choices when it comes to your options with variable annuity subaccounts. There are literally hundreds of ways to portion out your investment. The following are major subaccount choices and a little feedback is provided on how to go about selecting how much to put in and where to put it.

Aggressive: An aggressive subaccount is comprised largely of higher-risk investments. Here, the focus is on gaining as much capital as possible. This may be done through small cap stocks or even riskier products, such as foreign currencies or options. It is not a good idea to put a large percentage of your investment money into an aggressive account regardless of how comfortable you feel with the risk.

Balanced: This type of subaccount is for those looking for a well-rounded investment, usually blending aggressive subaccounts with more stable, growth-oriented investments.

Growth: Growth accounts are stable investments that offer very little in gains. Income is not a main focus in these types of investments; the focus is on preserving assets. Because of this, growth account fund managers may invest in the more reliant large cap stocks or corporate and government bonds.

Income: Income accounts look for investment products that offer small but steady gains. If your insurance company includes dividends in their accounts, these funds will be included. However, most insurance companies do not pay dividends, making straight income accounts an infrequent choice for annuity investors. Again, corporate and government bonds comprise a large percentage of income accounts.

Growth and Income: This type of account is also a stable investment, netting slightly more than simple growth accounts. Again, the focus of these accounts is not necessarily a large income, despite the name. Rather, the focus is on consistent and regular gains.

Bonds: Corporate bonds are amounts of money borrowed by corporations from either private or institutional investors. Because they are actually debts owed by a company and do not represent any degree of ownership, they are considered a much more stable investment. If a company goes under, bonds are repaid prior to stocks. Although bonds are much more stable than stock investments, they do not pay as much in returns. Remember, there is usually a trade-off between risk and return.

Metals: Precious metals are oftentimes invested in by speculators who distrust the abstract nature of the stock market. Gold is the most common metal invested in, but it is not the only one available. These types of investments are more common in mutual fund investments than they are in annuities.

Subaccounts

The above investment choices are further divided into subaccounts within your annuity. Subaccounts exist so you can diversify your portfolio, yet keep your money within the same company and even the same annuity. It is much easier to see what you have earned and lost when you have one statement that explains everything that happens side by side during a business cycle. For example, you might have 80 percent of your investment in a consistent and fairly safe growth subaccount, 15 percent in bonds and 5 percent in a more risky aggressive subaccount. Some insurance companies allow you to monitor and change your subaccounts online, while others require a phone call to your agent. Either way, the possible variations available to you are endless. Furthermore, all of these possibilities are available within the same insurance company and even within the same annuity contract.

It should be mentioned that you can freely exchange between these subaccounts. If you are not happy with the returns your growth and income variable annuity is getting, you can always transfer some or all of your money into a more aggressive subaccount. This transfer of funds should not be confused with a Section 1035 exchange, which is discussed in Chapter 12. The 1035 exchanges are meant for transferring money from one annuity to another. Subaccounts within the same annuity do not meet this criterion.

The transfer of money within the same annuity allows you to reposition assets so you can maximize your gains in good market times and minimize losses in poor market times. For example, the growth and income subaccount may earn 4.5 percent one quarter, while the aggressive subaccount returns 25 percent. When the investor receives his or her statement and sees this disparity, he or she may feel like repositioning assets to expose his or her money to the potential for higher returns. The next quarter, he or she may find that the growth and income subaccount again returned 4.5 percent because these are usually considered to be consistent and steady investments. Meanwhile, the aggressive subaccount may return only 10 percent during the next quarter. Although this is an improvement over the growth and income subaccount, it illustrates the point that aggressive investment strategies are less consistent.

Positioning large percentages of your investment in an aggressive account is frowned upon because of this fact.

You should always use more than one of the subaccounts offered. Diversification is extremely important, especially during unstable market times. By varying your investment risk classes, you not only protect yourself, but you will also maximize your returns over the long run.

In order to determine where the best place to put your money is, remember that money market accounts are considered the safest of subaccounts. They also are correspondingly the lowest netting over long periods. Bonds are a touch more risky, but they do offer statistically higher returns. Even more risky are the subaccounts that invest in the stock market. **Large cap stocks** are considered to be safer than **small cap stocks**. The fact that large cap stocks see more frequent trading action and higher dollar amounts makes them less vulnerable to swings in price. Small cap stocks, on the other hand, are not traded as frequently and are thus subject to the fluctuations caused by bigger trades.

Investing Styles

There are three major schools of thought when it comes to an individual's investing style. The first of these is the long-term buy and hold positions. These investors will divvy up their **capital** between the subaccounts they choose and then leave them there until retirement. Because the market has a general upward trend, this method is useful because it combats inflation. Rarely does this method beat inflation, though.

The second method is exercised by those who try to time their entry and exit positions into the market just right. This includes day traders, swing traders, and position traders. These individuals are labeled as traders rather than investors because of the increased frequency of their market transactions. It is a labor-intensive strategy with the potential for huge gains but also for huge losses. Many of these traders make their living simply by playing the stock market. They do not invest in annuities because these are considered long-term investments and have the penalty structure to enforce themselves as such.

In between these two extremes lies the short-term investor. These individuals do not check up on their investments daily, but they do not just buy and hold their investments either. Investors of this type will monitor their investments maybe once a month, making sure everything progresses how it should. By keeping their portfolios diverse and reallocating capital in the subaccounts at these regular intervals, this type of investor will see the most consistent increases in their investments.

Asset allocation

Your asset allocation should be a mirror image of your risk tolerance. A good rule of thumb is that your age should correspond to your percentage of conservative investments. For example, a 40-year-old would have 40 percent of his or her annuity in a more conservative amount and the remaining 60 percent in an aggressive account.

Whether your investment strategy is passive or aggressive though, it is important that your asset allocation match your tolerance. This may mean reallocating funds on a regular basis. Because different subaccounts will earn or lose different amounts, keeping your assets balanced correctly requires a degree of supervision. For example, a sample portfolio may contain 20 percent aggressive holdings, 20 percent cash accounts, and 60 percent balanced holdings. As the market rises and falls, the percentage points in each category will naturally shift. Your subaccounts operate independent of each other. If the aggressive subaccount performs particularly well, it may gain a higher percentage of space inside your portfolio. In the previous example, if the balanced account grew at a smaller pace than the aggressive account, the balanced account would go down in percentage, and the aggressive holdings would rise — even though they both were profitable. The end result may then look something like this: aggressive — 25 percent; balanced — 55 percent; and cash account — 20 percent.

There are a few things that can be done with this example. If your risk tolerance has changed, you might choose to do nothing. This would be the case if you are very pleased with how the aggressive portfolio has performed. Considering this, you may not be as adverse to the risk associated with such investments.

If your needs and risk tolerance have not changed, you will want to rearrange your portfolio so it matches your previous needs. Shifting money from the aggressive account back to the balanced account so they comprise their original 20 and 60 percent, respectively, will give you the best outcome.

This may seem counterintuitive at first. Why would you take money from a subaccount that is performing well and place it in a lesser performing subaccount? You would execute this transfer because of the need for diversification. If your risk class has not changed, you will want to reallocate assets so your portfolio's diversity remains intact and so it stays at the most beneficial level for you. The market can change at any time, and if you are a touch on the conservative side, you will want to protect your investment by shifting money back to the original allocation. Diversifying protects investors from a failing or a short-coming in any one sector or subaccount. Markets often seem to behave irrationally, and if you have not properly allocated your funds, you may see a huge and sudden loss in a particular zone of your investment that could take years to make up. Not all subaccounts will perform well each quarter, but if you are well diversified, you can protect yourself against this inevitability. Because the subaccounts are independent of each other, even if some of your investment loses money, not all is lost. If you have spread your money out wisely, losses will be minimized.

For example, a 30-year-old should have 30 percent in conservative investments and the remaining 70 percent in higher-risk accounts. The reasoning for this is simple: Stock markets have been proven to rise over long periods. This is one of the very few things that can be said as a maxim when dealing with the stock market. And, if a loss does occur, there is plenty of time to recoup losses and then some. The sample pie chart on the next page is one possible way that a 30-year-old might allocate his or her capital.

Asset Allocation for a 30-Year-Old

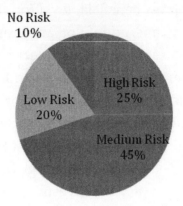

No Risk
10%

Low Risk
20%

High Risk
25%

Medium Risk
45%

An annuity could fall anywhere on this chart. Fixed annuities would be considered no- or low-risk investments, while variable annuities can be much riskier. An annuity, however, should not be used as a 30-year-old's high-risk investment for the simple fact that he or she cannot access that money until age 59½. If the market sours, he or she would not have the ability to take his or her money out of the market and keep it in cash holdings, a valuable hedging strategy.

On the other side of the coin, a 70-year-old should have 70 percent of his or her assets in a low- or no-risk account. This makes annuities much more appealing to the elderly than to a younger investor. This does not necessarily mean that the young should avoid annuities. Variable annuities are variable investments and have many benefits for younger investors, regardless of tax bracket.

As you approach your later years, you will see that it is not necessary to have any high-risk investments. High-risk holdings work best over a long period, and as you grow

Asset Allocation for a 70-Year-Old

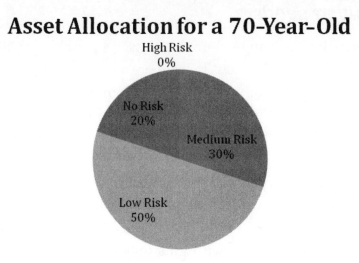

older, you will want your money where it is most easily accessible. The one reason why you should have any medium-risk holdings is so you can compete with inflation in the event you live longer than your expected age.

Inflation protection can be accomplished in a few ways:

- Stock investments

- Variable Annuities

- Advanced Life Deferred Annuities

An advanced life deferred annuity is considered a medium-risk investment because it is only available to those who live long enough, usually between ages 80 and 85. If you do not live to the predetermined age, your investment simply goes to the insurance company. This may not appeal to most, but for those who have longevity running in their family, this may be an appropriate choice.

Shifting needs

Time will also change your risk class. As people age, life-time events trigger new investment needs. Raising children, seeing them through college, paying for their weddings, and funding your own happy retirement full of travel and leisure all necessitate the reallocation of funds. Each individual's cycle of investments will be different, but normally, investment strategies start out fairly aggressive and become more conservative as time passes. Self-insuring techniques advocate the use of stocks and bonds, but variable annuities with guarantees attached to them can accomplish this for you because you will have total control over your subaccounts. Luckily, in tax-deferred accounts, transfers between subaccounts are not taxable. There are even some variable funds out there that will automatically shift your investment allocation as you age.

Fees

Variable annuities are more transparent with the fees charged to annuity owners than fixed annuities. The fees are determined by which type of subaccount you choose and average around 2 percent of the amount invested. International and aggressive accounts charge the highest management fees, while the lower-risk accounts charge less. This is because aggressive accounts involve more vigilance and thus more work on the end of the company managing your money. Low-risk accounts, such as a money market account, involve less time and work to manage.

Fees can quickly add up, especially with deferred variable annuities. The more fees you are charged, the less money there is for your retirement. With variable annuities, there is no way around these fees because brokers are the ones selling these, and they need to be paid somehow. Commission charges account for the bulk of the fees associated with variable annuities. They are also more labor intensive than a fixed annuity. Because of this, these annuities charge a load fee, an amount taken right out of your principal at the time of purchase. The additional fees for variable annuities come with some benefits, though. The investor will most likely receive advice from a broker or adviser. For those new or unfamiliar to the world of investing, this can be extremely valuable. Those investors who are experienced will also be able to actively manage their funds because of the flexibility of the subaccounts. In addition, the investor may be eligible for guaranteed living benefits, such as principal bonuses or minimum accumulation rights.

A common charge is the front-end load fee, or A-share. This is a percentage of your investment that is skimmed off the top. If the charge is for 3 percent and you have a $100,000 investment, it would mean $3,000 less would gain interest right from the beginning.

The B-share fee is perhaps the most widely used assessment when it comes to variable annuities. Rather than being taken out at the beginning of the contract's life, B-shares execute a charge on early withdrawals. Charges start at 7 or 8 percent for the first year, then diminish over the next several years of the contract. Within five to seven years, the fee will drop down to 0 percent.

Luckily, there are alternatives to these high fees out there. No-load annuities exist with companies like Vanguard® or

T. Rowe Price®. These no-load annuities do not charge an upfront sales charge, meaning the entire principal starts gaining interest right away. These are commonly referred to as C-share annuities. With no-load annuities, you will not have to play catch up for the first few years of the contract because no fees will be deducted from your account balance.

Some annuities have what are known as a wrap fee. These accounts do not have a clear-cut commission charge; rather, the company will bill the account owner on an annual basis to cover the costs of money management.

Another rarely used fee is the L-share. These annuities have shorter surrender periods than the B-share annuities do but charge a higher mortality and expense fee. The mortality and expense fee has proven to be a great money-maker for insurance companies. This fee is a percentage of the balance within the account. Sometimes this rate can be as high as 2 percent. While 2 percent may not seem like a great deal, consider the fact that inflation has taken place at a historic rate of 3 percent per year. When you subtract the mortality and expense fees, an average performance will only see a growth of 1 percent per year, which is hardly enough to make your investment worthwhile. L-share annuities should be avoided because of this.

Regardless of the type of partial account you choose to invest in, each subaccount of your variable annuity has a fund manager who oversees the daily performance of your investment. That manager needs to get paid somehow, and not surprisingly, his or her salary comes from your fees. These are referred to as investment management fees and vary depending on how aggressive your allocation is. As a general rule, the more aggressive the investment, the higher the fee.

Other features of variable annuities

The prospectus

The **prospectus** is a piece of literature that contains a list of the different subaccounts available for the variable annuity in question. By law, any variable account must give a brief description of the goals of each subaccount and how it attempts to achieve those goals. These are normally limited to funds within the company you are applying through but will sometimes include mutual funds from other companies, as well as points of comparison. You will want to look over these subaccounts carefully and find a combination that meets your needs. It is also worth your while to inquire how these subaccounts have performed in the past. You will only want to choose subaccounts that have a successful history, although you do want to make sure they have been successful over a long period. Your insurance agent should have records available, if he or she has been around for a while, as to the return over the last year, the last three years, and the last ten years. You will want to consider all of these before making your decision. Because your annuity will be a long-term investment, you should give the longer periods more weight when making your decision.

The prospectus will also include a goal or objective for each subaccount listed. Although goals are oftentimes quite generic, you will want to pay special attention to the methods used for achieving goals. This is where you will determine whether the "balanced" subaccount is truly

balanced. The specific holdings and investments made —
and not made — will be listed here. Make sure the subaccount you choose lives up to its risk class.

Sample Prospectus:

#1 Insurance Agency

      Maximum Growth Account Prospectus

      Net Assets: $10.7 Million

      Returns: 1 Year: +5.9%

                  5 Years: -1.0%

                  10 Years: +3.4%

      Share Value: 1995: $10

                  2000: $15

                  2005: $25

      Adviser: John Q. Public

      Dividends: Added each December, if applicable.

      Qualified?: Yes

      Inception Date: December 20, 1994

      Ticker Symbol: MGAP

The prospectus should be relatively straightforward if you
know where to look. The prospectus can be a long docu-
ment; some are up to 50 pages long. Oftentimes though,
the information you are looking for can be found on one
or two pages. In the fictional example above, you can see
how much money is invested in the fund, what the rates
of return over the last one, five, and ten years has been,
what one share of the fund costs, who manages the fund,
and what symbol the fund is listed as. Most prospectuses
are many pages long; you may have to sift through dozens

of pages of information to find what you are looking for. By knowing what is important, you can more easily make your decision.

This is where you will get to know the manager overseeing your account. A brief biography and details of his or her experience will be listed. Fees and added charges will be reported here as well.

Guaranteed minimum death benefit

This is a key feature in some variable annuities that will guarantee a return for your beneficiary in the event you pass away during the accumulation period. With this feature, your principal amount is normally completely guaranteed, although sometimes the entire contract value is guaranteed — minus any withdrawals of course. In this case, the annuity money is received free of probate. Your heir is held responsible for the taxes on any gains the account has seen. The guaranteed minimum death benefit rider may come at a cost to the owner. This may be a set price or a percentage of the initial investment.

Risk reduction

In order to meet your needs, you should choose the level of risk that most accurately matches your stage in life and the corresponding goals. As explained before, your tolerance for risk should naturally decrease as you age. Your variable annuity can change alongside you if you monitor it. Like any good investor, you should always be aware of where your money is. The flexible premium variable annuity you opened when you were 40 is not appropriate for you at age 70. This means that the 70 percent aggressive/30 percent growth portfolio that was recommended to you earlier on in life is not the same variable annuity you should have when you retire.

Risk can always be reduced as long as you have a variable annuity that allows you to change the risk classes of your investment during the life of the contract. Avoid variable annuities that do not allow you to do so. Your risk tolerance will change as you age, and your annuity should be able to as well. If you do not feel comfortable changing your asset structure, your agent should be able to provide the help necessary to meet your needs.

Annuitizing a Variable Contract

When you annuitize your variable annuity, your monthly distribution will fluctuate up or down along with the value of your subaccounts. If you have chosen a straight life, a joint and survivor option, or any other option that guarantees you income for the entirety of your life, your money will hopefully continue to grow in these accounts, even as you withdraw from them. The rate at which your subaccounts grow during this period depends on what your asset allocation looks like, how much you wish to receive per month, and of course, how the market performs. Even though you are enjoying your retirement at this point, you may still want to routinely manage your subaccounts in order to have the biggest distributions possible.

Advantages of a variable annuity

There are many advantages to variable annuities. It is quite possible for a variable annuity to make as much as 20 percent or more during the course of a year. This does not mean it will occur every year, but with a variable annuity, you could see large returns over the course of many years during your contract. No investment can make returns this large year after year, and there is no way of knowing how a variable account will perform in the future, but it is possibly in theory.

Another major advantage is that with variable annuities, owners have the opportunity to allocate their funds exactly the way they desire. In poor market times, this can mean holding more of an investor's money in cash accounts, while during good times, the investor can switch to a more aggressive blend.

Perhaps the most attractive aspect of variable annuities is their guaranteed living benefits. Most annuities have death benefits, but living benefits are a relatively new phenomenon. These are essentially riders that add value to the annuitant's situation while they live. Besides the added perks that some guaranteed living benefits provide, these riders give the investor more control over their money. Guaranteed living benefits are covered in greater detail in Chapter 8 under product features.

Variable annuities, according to a study conducted by John P. Huggard, have lower costs and fees than mutual funds, another factor that makes them a superior investment. You will also accomplish something else with variable annuities that you cannot get out of a mutual fund: no capital gains taxes. With a mutual fund, managers will buy and sell stocks on a regular basis, causing a capital gains tax charge that will more than likely be handed down to the investor. Variable annuities are not charged with any taxes until withdrawals begin.

Disadvantages of a variable annuity

Variable annuities are at the mercy of the market. As you are aware, the stock market moves in cycles. Although the overall trend of the stock market is upward, years of progress can be erased in a few months. This can be partially avoided by selecting less risky subaccounts, but you will also see less-than-average gains during good market times. This is actually a hidden positive of a variable annuity, as you do have the freedom to move around your subaccounts and amounts allocated in them. Consider an average year where a hypothetical variable annuity gains 5 percent overall. The funds in this annuity were allocated 50 percent in cash accounts, 20 percent in growth accounts, and 30 percent in an aggressive account. If the fund was worth $100,000 at the beginning of the year, it would have had $50,000 in cash accounts, $20,000 in growth accounts, and $30,000 in the aggressive account. It would now be worth $105,000. But, suppose each account had actually declined in value with the cash account being the exception. Because of asset allocation, the hypothetical investor in this example made money, even when the general market fell in price.

With variable annuities, there is also the risk that your principal amount may shrink. Unless you have a guaranteed living benefit, this is a very real possibility if you do not invest your money for the long term. Short-term investments will almost always feel the wrath of high surrender charges.

Variable annuities also tend to have higher maintenance and commission charges than their fixed counterparts. There are variable annuities out there that also have higher rates than mutual funds. Sometimes, this rate can be as high as 2 percent of your total investment. This makes variable annuities more useful as a longer-term invest-ment when compared to these two other products.

But, variable annuities are not as easy to comprehend as fixed annuities. If you are looking for something you can park your money in and forget about until you need it, you may want to consider a fixed annuity because of its ease of understanding for the investor.

Market timing also plays a role in the success of variable annuities. If your primary deposit into a variable account occurs at the beginning of a bad fiscal year, it can take years of catching up to get back on track. Although the overall trend of the market is upward, each year does not necessarily follow suit, making these types of investments much more beneficial over longer periods.

How to Tell if this is the Right Type of Annuity for Me

Variable annuities are good for people investing for much further down the road. Because you can choose your risk class, they make for great retirement vessels, especially if you purchase a flexible premium variable annuity. The flexible premiums allow you to contribute money into the account when you can. There is no limit to what you can contribute to an annuity, as there are with IRAs.

If you are considering investing your money in a mutual fund, a variable annuity might better suit your needs. Not only do they have lower costs associated with them, but they also perform just as well as mutual funds.

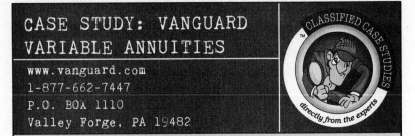

The Vanguard Group offers some of the best annuity products on the market and for good reason. Many Vanguard agents do not work by commission, meaning they make money regardless of whether they sell you anything or not. This fact allows agents to make unbiased decisions; they are not going to simply sell you a high-fee product just so they can make the most amount of money off you.

Vanguard's variable annuity charges are 75 percent less than the national average within the insurance industry, as stated on their website (**www.vanguard.com**). Their portfolio touts a wide array of funds, ranging from a money market subaccount to more aggressive small company subaccounts.

The small company fund had a year-to-date growth of more than 30 percent, as of October 2009. With accessibility a key factor in the company's continued success, they even have a Web page where you can open up your annuity online; all that it takes is about ten minutes of work on your part.

Vanguard recommends opening a variable annuity if you are already contributing the maximum allowed to both a 401(k) and an IRA account and you want or need additional savings. They also suggest you should only begin an annuity contract if you have five years or more left in the workforce until you plan on retiring. This is simply so you can get the most out of your investment and avoid any surrender charges.

They also make a 1035 exchange (which will be discussed in Chapter 12) as painless as possible. In addition to comparing surrender charges and other fees and expenses, Vanguard will even help you fill out the paperwork. Most attractive of all, Vanguard ranks no lower than an "A" in each of the major insurance company review sites.

If you do encounter trouble while filling out an application or if you just have a question or two, you can call a Vanguard agent and he or she can walk you through the process.

Key Features of Variable Annuities

- Variable annuities can be tailored to meet an individual's needs much more easily than a fixed annuity.

- Transfers between subaccounts are easy and will help keep your investment relevant to your needs.

- Variable annuities offer greater gains than fixed annuities.

- There is a trade-off between risk and return, though. The higher the return, the higher the degree of risk. Although variable annuities can gain more than fixed annuities, they can also lose money.

- Variable annuities are better for younger investors because they keep up with the rate of inflation. Fixed annuities, although they have a solid guarantee, may lose spending power over long periods.

Chapter 6

Equity-indexed annuities are a type of fixed annuity that are connected to a market index. Standard & Poor's 500 Composite Stock Price Index — S&P 500 — is one of the most commonly used indices. The purchaser of an equity-indexed annuity is not buying shares in a stock or an index; this type of annuity is still considered an insurance contract. They are also considered fixed annuities because they have a set minimum interest rate they will pay even if the market dips below that set rate. If the market thrives, however, a predetermined formula, known as the participation rate, will determine how much interest is credited to your annuity. Formulas differ from company to company but are described as a percentage of their particular market's overall gain.

Basic Facts

Annuities in this category offer a little bit of each of the previously discussed types of annuities, whether they are fixed or variable. Their main purpose is to provide more lucrative returns than a fixed annuity while still protecting the principal investment. When stocks rise, these annuities will offer higher rates. When they fall, they offer the bare minimum, which is stipulated in the contract. In the vast majority of cases, you cannot lose money with this type of annuity.

Although formulas vary between companies in regards to the amount earned during good market times, the average increase is about 50 percent of whatever the market rises. For instance, if the market rises 10 percent during the course of a year, your $100,000 initial investment will rise by 5 percent, or $5,000.

Take a look at another realistic example. Assume the market drops 5 percent this time. If you have a guaranteed rate of 2 percent, your $100,000 investment would now be $102,000. The same investment with a variable annuity would have dropped down to $95,000 — a difference of $7,000.

Just remember that the opposite is true as well. In the first example, the $100,000 would have risen to $110,000. The equity-indexed annuity would have been $5,000 less because it only rises 50 percent of whatever rate the market rises at.

With equity-indexed annuities, your choices are not the same as variable annuities when it comes to how your risk classification is divvied up. There are no subaccounts when dealing with this type of annuity. The majority of your money is invested in the bond market, where it is virtually guaranteed a profit. The rest of the money, minus any applicable fees, is put into an **index option**. An index is basically a group of similar companies. The most prominent of these is the Dow Jones Industrial Average (DJIA). The companies contained within the DJIA are various, but they are grouped together because they lead their respective industry.

Options, on the other hand, give the insurance company the choice to purchase or sell something, such as a stock, bond, or commodity. These options are a somewhat risky way to purchase things. If the price of the index goes up, the company buys it at a discount. If the price drops below the option price, however, the company can choose to negate the contract and only lose its options fee. An option is a right to buy or sell and not a mandatory requirement. This allows the company to make money in one direction — up — and lose just a little when the market sours.

Unlike variable annuities, you cannot diversify your money in whichever way you wish. There is not an option to invest in stocks, merely to invest in indices and bonds. This is done automatically by the insurance company in order to serve the investor with a layer of protection; indices are far more stable than an individual stock because they represent a larger aspect of the market.

Indexing Methods

There are four major methods in which market gains are credited to your account. Listed below is an explanation of each one.

Annual Reset: Values of the market index are compared twice a year by the insurance company — once at the beginning of the contract year and once at the end. Interest is then added to your account accordingly at the end of each year, as determined by your participation rate. The interest earned is added to the balance of the annuity and cannot go down.

For example, if the Dow Jones Industrial Average is at 10,000 points when you purchase your equity-indexed annuity, and one year later it is at 10,500, the market will have seen a 5 percent increase. With a participation rate of 80 percent, your investment will see a rise of 80 percent of that 5 percent increase. A $100,000 investment then would see a gain of $4,000. From that point on, the annuity's value cannot fall below $104,000 regardless of how the market performs in subsequent years.

High-Water Mark: Market indices are observed at several points during the term of your annuity under this method. This occurs on or around the anniversary of your contract and is determined once per year. Interest is determined by comparing the highest of these various observations with the original index value. If there is a **look-back option** with this type of indexing method, it simply means the insurance company will search backward each year to find the highest point the particular index reached.

Again, assume the Dow was at 10,000 points at the beginning of the contract. At the end of the first year, the Dow is still at 10,000 for a seemingly gain of zero. However, if the high-water mark with a look-back option is used, the insurance company will backtrack throughout the course of the year and see that at one point, the Dow actually read 11,000 points. If there is an 80 percent participation rate, the 10 percent gain the market saw will be cut down to an 8 percent gain for the annuity. A $100,000 investment would increase to $108,000, even though the market ended right where it began the year.

Low-Water Mark: This indexing method is similar to the high-water mark method. The main difference is that rather than selecting the highest valued observation of the index, the lowest value is considered. Interest, if any, is then added appropriately. This is not the best option for an investor. If the market is volatile during the given period, it may result in a low interest rate when the market has actually risen overall. By comparing different products, you can avoid this type of crediting method.

To illustrate this point, refer to the hypothetical 10,000-point Dow to begin with once more. Throughout the course of the year, the index will be observed at certain times. Even if the Dow ends the year at 12,000 points for a gain of 20 percent, if one of the observation points reads 10,500 points, only 5 percent will be used to calculate the increase in the amount of the equity-indexed annuity. Again, with an 80 percent participation rate, a $100,000 investment will increase to $104,000 rather than the $116,000 that a high-water mark method would end with.

Point-to-Point: The interest in point-to-point indexing is earned by comparing the index value once at the beginning of the term and then again at the end of the contract's term. The amount earned during that period is calculated by subtracting the final value from the starting value. Interest is then added to the account all at once at the conclusion of the term. This method is quite similar to the annual reset method, except that it takes out the volatility because only two numbers are used, the beginning and the end. The annual reset takes into account the ups and downs that may happen year to year. Because of this, the point-to-point method of crediting is superior.

A point-to-point crediting method works best for long-term investments. The Dow has increased drastically over the course of the last 50 years. If the Dow was at 10,000 points when the annuity was purchased and 30 years later, the index is at 15,000 points, it will have increased by 50 percent. An 80 percent participation rate will net a 40 percent increase for the annuity, bringing a $100,000 annuity up to $140,000.

Additional features of equity-indexed annuities

There are several features that add or subtract from the value of equity-indexed annuities. Some of them come automatically with your contract while others may be optional. It is important you know which features are most beneficial to your contract, and even more important, you fully understand the factors influencing the annuity.

Interest Capping: This feature will actually set a limit to how much interest your annuity can earn. Although this is a negative, annuities with this type of feature will often include annual earning updates and the ability to take partial distributions. A partial distribution gives the investor the ability to safely withdraw a specified amount from their annuity without actually exercising the distribution aspect of the contract. It also allows investors to work around surrender periods.

Averaging: Averaging is the process of finding the mean within a market during a specific period, usually a year, and applying that mean to the annuity's interest-earning formula. This feature is meant to prevent you from purchasing your annuity during a market high, which would greatly reduce the amount of interest your annuity would earn during the first year. Although this feature is meant to protect you, it can work in the opposite direction: If the market suddenly rises toward the end of your term, your interest earned will not reflect it as much because the market's average is what is used to determine the final amount of interest.

For example, consider a market that sits stagnant for most of the year. When there are market increases, they are immediately negated the next day by a drop in market prices. Then, finally, after 11 months of churning, the market breaks out of its range, and investors start to see real positive growth. If you had a market averaging crediting system in place, your account would only grow by $\frac{1}{12}$ of what the market actually increased by. If the market grew by 1,200 points during the last month, only 100 would be credited to your account. This is because an averaging crediting method would look at 11 months of 0-percent growth and weight the one month of actual growth accordingly.

Participation Rate: The participation rate is the formula used to calculate how a rise in the market index will affect index-connected interest. For example, if the participation rate is 75 percent, and the market rises by 10 percent, then your annuity will rise 7.5 percent because 10 percent of 75 is 7.5. Participation rates may vary from year to year within the same company. It is important to note the current participation rate for each year of your annuity because of the fact that these rates may vary from year to year.

Good to Know:

Some companies will set limits as to how high their participation rate will go. If unlimited growth is your goal, this is something you will want to avoid. The opposite is also true; companies may set a limit as to how low the participation rate can drop. This will protect the investor from missing out on market gains. Make sure you ask an agent to explain the company's current and future participation rates to you. Low participation rates in a good economy can severely limit how much your annuity earns.

Margin or Spread Fees: You may not make all of the interest the selected index earns. This is commonly known as a margin or spread fee, and is an alternative to the participation rate. For example, the company may choose to lower your earned interest rate 2 percentage points below what the index actually earns. If the index earns 10 percent over the course of the year, you will have 8 percent credited to your account. This occurs in lieu of a participation rate. Insurance companies utilize this method because it guarantees a larger profit for the company when the market performs well.

Floor on Interest: This is the minimum index-related interest rate you will earn. In most cases, the floor will be set at 0 percent, meaning that even if the market dips into the negatives, you will earn zero interest rather than lose money. This will protect your principal investment, and after the first year, it will protect interest earned from year to year. Since equity-indexed annuities are fixed, your annuity will have a guaranteed minimum value it cannot fall below.

Interest Compounding: You want to make sure your equity-indexed annuity pays compound interest. Some annuities of this type pay **simple interest**, meaning only the principal amount earns interest during an index term. With **compound interest**, your interest will earn its own interest as well. Steer clear of simple interest annuities — they seriously inhibit the annuity's earning potential.

Dividends: Many stocks pay dividends to their shareholders if they perform especially well over the course of the fiscal year. A dividend is a sum of money that companies will pay out to their shareholders if the stock performs exceptionally well. Depending on the index, this may or may not be reflected in the index's price. For example, the S&P 500 recognizes only stock values; dividends paid out are not recognized in annuities tied to this index. This may actually harm equity-indexed annuity owners. During efficient market times, stock prices may drop accordingly after a dividend has been paid out. This is due to the fact that the net worth of a company inherently drops after it pays its dividends out to each shareholder.

Vesting: The vesting period is the length of time you must have your account before earnings will be accredited. Some companies will credit index-related earnings to your account only if the money is kept in the annuity account for the entire term stipulated in the contract. If money is withdrawn early, the company may credit only some of the interest earned. Some companies may even completely withhold earnings in the event of an early withdrawal of your principal amount. Make sure you are aware of any vesting periods spelled out in your contract.

Cap Rate: The cap rate is the maximum rate of return the contract will be given. If there is a cap rate of 15 percent, even if the index the annuity is connected to performs amazingly well and returns 50 percent, the annuity will still only rise by the 15 percent spelled out in the contract. Again, the rate the annuity raises at is still determined by the participation rate. Cap rates merely put a limit as to how much the annuity will rise in value. This method protects the insurance company from paying large amounts of interest to their annuities and hurts investors more than it helps them.

Advantages of equity indexed annuities

Equity-indexed annuities offer the best of both worlds in terms of fixed and variable. There is a minimum interest rate guaranteed during rough market times, which is the beneficial aspect of a fixed annuity. At the same time, you are still eligible to profit from upswings in the economy, which is the most beneficial aspect of a variable annuity. Risk budgeting is a key advantage. This protects the investor from any downswings in the economy with a guaranteed minimum rate of return. Even though the return guarantee is often 0 percent, this is a promise that variable annuities cannot make. It also is a way to ensure your investment does not lose money.

The best equity-indexed annuities offer flexibility. Some will allow you to choose which index or indices you want your account to mirror, how you want your surrender period structured, and how you want your account credited. These relatively new advances in equity-indexed annuities are definitely an advantage.

Index funds are considered to be much safer places to put your money than other types of investments. This reputation is well earned; index funds provide an automatic diversification to your portfolio. Because an index covers dozens, if not hundreds, of stocks, the risk is already spread out for you. Although some people equate playing the stock market with gambling, index funds are the safer bet.

Disadvantages of equity indexed annuities

The disadvantages of equity-indexed annuities are quite similar to their advantages. You are combining the features of the two main types of annuities, and this can lead to watered-down profits. During good market times, you only gain a small amount of what a variable annuity would make. During recessions, you will be stuck with a low minimum. Although you are hopefully making more than a fixed annuity during good market times, you will be making less than a fixed annuity during bad times.

Overall, the rate of return is very difficult to ascertain with this type of annuity; even your broker will not be able to give you an exact number, only historical performances. Even then, you will not have a clear idea of how your investment will perform. This is mainly because indexed annuities are a newer type of annuity. First used in the United States in 1996, these annuities are still evolving. Although there are many good indexed annuities out there, the best are still yet to come.

How to Tell if Equity-indexed Annuities Are Right for Me

Equity-indexed annuities offer a bit more risk than fixed annuities but are not as volatile as variable annuities. Like anything linked to an index or stock performance, it is impossible to completely predict how that particular set of investments will act. Most equity-indexed annuities will guarantee your principal amount and even offer a low guaranteed rate. In good market years, they will offer even better returns. But, these returns will not compare to the returns of a variable annuity during good market years.

Is a guaranteed minimum interest rate important to you? Do you want the possibility of earning more than the minimum? Equity-indexed annuities may not be as high-profile as variable annuities, but they do serve a purpose. Your principal will be protected, and there is more long-term potential for earnings than in a fixed annuity. The biggest drawback to these annuities, however, is they are still in the early years of being developed. As the kinks are worked out, newer equity-indexed annuity contracts will probably improve upon earlier ones.

If you are considering the purchase of a mutual fund, this type of annuity might be a more appropriate choice. Indexed annuities offer the same key benefit that mutual funds do: diversification of funds. This comes with a guarantee; something no mutual fund can promise you.

Colleen King is an insurance broker in Northridge, Calif., where she focuses mainly on health insurance, both for individuals and groups. Because she works in the insurance field, she knows how important it is to be prepared for the future. King owns two annuities, both of which are equity-indexed annuities. Although these annuities are connected to a market index, they are technically fixed annuities because they are guaranteed never to fall below a certain percentage rate of return. Like most other equity-indexed annuities, that rate of return is 0 percent for King.

Why is 0 percent an attractive option? Prior to purchasing the annuities, King had her money mainly in stock holdings. When the stock market crashed in 2008, King and other investors saw a huge decrease in the value of their holdings. Some of her accounts fell by as much as 60 percent. By purchasing an indexed annuity, although the annuity will not increase in value, it is guaranteed not to fall into the negative as so many other investments do.

King chose to go through Allianz, who offered her a 12-percent bonus on any funds added to the annuities within the first five years. Ordinarily, the bonus they offer is only 10 percent, but thanks to the hard times that the economy is having, they have raised the rate to attract business. For King, that seems to be working. Even if the market declines, the bonus rate keeps the equity-indexed annuities performing well.

King stressed that annuities are a long-term investment. Surrender periods can last upward of eight to ten years, if money is drawn out before that period, a portion of the investment will disappear. Insurance companies do this so they can make a profit. By keeping some money in more liquid accounts, such as stocks, bonds, and real estate, King has found a nice balance.

Still, King stresses that annuities are not appropriate for everyone. "You don't put a 75 year old into a ten, or maybe even a 15-year, surrender period product," King said. "There's a lot more to take into consideration on this." Money for emergencies should also not be kept in an annuity. While annuities offer penalty-free withdrawals of 10 percent, they are the last place investors should turn to for emergency funds, she says.

Key Points to Remember

- Equity-indexed annuities combine key features of both variable and fixed annuities. Although this type of annuity fluctuates according to the market, they still have a fixed rate they cannot fall below, usually 0 percent.

- The participation rate can make or break the contract. A normal participation rate is 80 percent, meaning that 80 percent of whatever gains the market sees will be credited to your account. If the market increases by 10 percent, only an 8 percent gain will be seen.

Chapter 7

Tax-sheltered Annuities

Tax-sheltered annuities, identified in the Internal Revenue Code as 403(b) plans, are common retirement investments for people working in the not-for-profit sector. Upon starting a tax-sheltered annuity, you have the freedom to decide whether you want a fixed or variable account. They operate quite similarly to regular annuities, except that a tax-sheltered annuity receives special treatment under tax laws that its public counterpart, the 401(k), does not. Enacted into law in 1958, 403(b) plans are beneficial because the premiums are deducted from paychecks before taxes are, making contributions to them tax deductible. If you work within the nonprofit sector, a tax-sheltered annuity will benefit you in ways that other annuities cannot.

Who is Eligible?

The most common recipients of tax-sheltered annuities are public school teachers. If you are a full-time employee in a nonprofit school system, you will qualify for a 403(b) plan. Other nonprofit employees can also invest in these annuities, such as local government employees, religious clergy, and hospital workers. Priests and ministers, however, normally do not qualify for these plans because they are considered independent contractors. In short, if the company you work for has tax-exempt status, odds are you are eligible for a 403(b). If your employer does not offer you a retirement plan, you should approach your human resources department. They may be able to start a company-wide retirement plan for you. At the very least, your human resources department will point you in the right direction and help you get a retirement savings plan started.

Group or individual?

The 403(b) plans are group plans, meaning they must be set up through an employer. The contract is thus between the insurance company and the employer. This does not hinder them from having a degree of individuality, though. With most companies, you can elect to have your tax-sheltered annuity become a variable annuity through an insurance company or invest it in a custodial account comprised of mutual funds. The latter is established through Internal Revenue Code 403(b)(7) and is basically an annuity tied to a mutual fund's performance. Participation in these different plans is determined by the employer; oftentimes, especially in small rural school districts, there is little to no choice for employees.

Individual 403(b) plans do exist, although they are less common. In this instance, the investor would be the signee on the contract rather than their employer. Individual contracts offer much more flexibility than group contracts. Individual plans occur when the investor leaves his or her job, making them able to take the tax-sheltered annuity with them They may either wait to take distributions upon hitting retirement age, rollover the money to an IRA, or bring the old tax-sheltered annuity to a new employer. This last option assumes that the new employer will be able to carry the old annuity. There are no taxes charged for these options until withdrawals begin.

Because 403(b)s are contributed to on a pre-tax basis, they are considered qualified plans. This reduces current income tax rates for recipients because contributions take place prior to the withdrawal of income taxes. This is especially beneficial if the investor falls into a lower tax bracket during their retirement years.

Crediting interest

There are two methods of crediting interest to your tax-sheltered annuity account that the insurance company might use: **portfolio averages** and **banding**.

The portfolio average method is a mirror of how the insurance company's investment portfolio holds up. If the insurance company has a good year so will its annuity holders. The portfolio average method looks at the investment as a whole and grows and shrinks with current market conditions.

The banding method credits money to accounts on a year-to-year basis only, based on the yield of each particular year. For example, the current year's contributions may have earned 10 percent, while previous years' contributions only earned 5 percent. The banding method groups only funds invested during a particular year, meaning parts of your investment will earn different interest rates. The banding method is most profitable when interest rates are rising. When interest rates are declining, the portfolio average method tends to be most beneficial to the investor because the investments have a greater degree of diversification.

Contributions

Like 401(k)s, 403(b) plans have employer matching incentives. About 70 percent of contributions made to tax-sheltered annuities are by the employee, and the other 30 percent made by the employer. In most cases, employees can contribute a certain amount from each paycheck, with the employer matching it up to a certain amount. The insurance company and the nonprofit company management dictate contribution parameters.

Another way to contribute to a 403(b) plan is by transferring money between accounts with a Section 1035 exchange. If an employee has another annuity somewhere, he or she is allowed to transfer that money when changing employers or if he or she is unhappy with a previous investment.

Loans

Many companies will allow you to take loans from your tax-sheltered annuity. There are, however, several restrictions you should know. Loans of $10,000 or more are taxable if your account is less than $20,000. If the account is greater than $20,000, and if the loan accounts for 50 percent or more, it is also taxable. These loans also must be repaid within a five-year period. If the loan is not repaid within that time, it is considered immediately taxable. By law, insurance companies are to notify the IRS of defaulted loans. Some insurance companies place safeguards on loans to prevent any unintended defaults.

Some insurance agents will use the fact that loans can be taken out of a 403(b) as ammunition in completing a sale. The argument used is that 403(b) plans are contributed to with pre-tax dollars. If an appropriate amount is borrowed, then that money can be used to pay off high-interest loans, such as credit card debt. This seems like a great strategy, right?

Well, it is not quite that simple. If the loan is not repaid within the five-year time frame, it is taxable and may be subject to a 10 percent penalty. Also, loan repayment is very strict. Missing just one payment can lead to default, causing interest rates on the amount to be repaid to spike drastically and for the IRS to become involved with the repayment process. It also locks the borrower in with the original annuity company until the loan is repaid. Annuitants can, in other situations, switch companies with a Section 1035 exchange, but any annuities that have had loans taken out cannot be exchanged. True, it is a nice option to have, but the potential consequences of taking out a loan should be seriously considered.

Fees

Like other annuities, tax-sheltered annuities are not managed for free. There are several sizeable fees attached to 403(b) plans. In fact, each deposit into the plan may be charged a small fee by the insurance company. This adds up quickly if the nonprofit worker is paid biweekly, as most teachers are. The manager overseeing the funds may also charge maintenance fees on a yearly basis in addition to the biweekly fee.

Payouts

With typical annuities, insurance companies will distribute less to females per distribution because they tend to live, on average, five years longer than men. The extra years of income are supposed to replace the excess distribution amounts that men receive. Regardless of this, employers are legally obligated to pay the same rate to men as to women because of workplace discrimination laws.

This is accomplished through a mixture of the rates calculated for each sex separately. Although this benefits female employees, it hampers men's earnings. One way around this is to roll over the account into a qualified IRA where it is no longer subject to the laws pertaining to employers. This way, the male investor can boost his earning power. Women will not want to do this in order to keep their distribution rates artificially higher, and thus get more out of their annuity.

This, of course, is subject to the particular state's insurance laws. In Montana, for example, sex discrimination in retirement program payouts of any kind is illegal so transferring an annuity makes no difference in distribution amounts. Aside from this type of discrimination, tax-sheltered annuities act just like regular variable annuities.

Selecting the Right Policy

Oftentimes, a school board committee will approve a very narrow array of products available to their employees.

Sometimes, it is the teachers' union that selects the products prior to board approval. If the union members are compensated for their plan selections in any way, their method of selection may be compromised. What does this mean to the average employee? It could mean your 403(b) is not as competitive as it should be. Plans with high maintenance costs should be avoided, as they gouge into the profits that would be returned to you upon retirement. Unfortunately, this does happen. Because nonprofit organizations have such limited choices when it comes to retirement products, they can be victimized with a narrow product line.

This limits your choices for exchanges. Although you are employed by the nonprofit, you can only invest in company-approved plans.

Advantages

Employers select 403(b) plans for their employees in order to help them save for retirement. In order to facilitate this, employers will often make contributions to a 403(b) alongside employees. This can be either a fixed amount each pay cycle or a percentage match of what the employee contributes. Because of this, a 403(b) is a valuable tool for anyone who is eligible to participate because it will grow much more quickly because of employer matching.

Another advantage to 403(b)s is the fact that the investor can choose between putting his or her money in a variable annuity or mutual funds. This may differ from employer to employer based on availability in the area, however. If it is available, it can be a good way to avoid higher fees and lower-performing products.

Pre-tax contributions are much more beneficial than post-tax dollar contributions when it comes to investing. With employer matching, 403(b) plans are one of the best investments available. If you have the opportunity to take advantage of a 403(b), you should do so by all means.

Disadvantages

The 403(b) plans, because they are for the nonprofit sector, oftentimes do not have all of the same accoutrements that 401(k) plans have. True, employers are allowed to contribute, but their matching limits are normally lower than a 401(k) plan would be because there is simply not as much discretionary money available to the nonprofit company.

Employers in the nonprofit sector do not have the same advisement structure available to 401(k) investors, especially in small and rural public school districts. With limited choices available, teachers in these situations need to be very aware of their investment options and the repercussions of those choices. Participating in a below-average plan can cause damage to a retirement nest egg that may take years to repair.

If investors chooses to invest their money in a mutual fund connected to their 403(b), they may be subject to higher fees. One of these is the **contingent-deferred sales charge**. This fee is determined by a percentage of the amount of shares purchased. The fee disappears if you hold your shares for a certain amount of time, usually ten years. This ensures investors are using their 403(b) strictly for retirement.

How to Tell if this is the Right Type of Annuity for Me

It is pretty easy to determine if 403(b) plans are appropriate. If you work in the nonprofit sector and earn enough money to set some aside for retirement, you should almost always invest in your employer-sponsored plan. There are rare occasions when it would be more beneficial to abstain from your company's plan and put your money elsewhere. If your employer-sponsored plan has extremely high fees, your money would probably be better off in a low-fee IRA account.

CASE STUDY: TIAA-CREF

www.tiaa-cref.org
1-800-842-2252
P.O. BOX 1259
Charlotte, NC 28201

TIAA-CREF is the nation's largest 403(b) plan provider. Their website offers a wide range of investment and insurance products. Each of the mutual funds and annuities sold through TIAA-CREF are free of sales charges, meaning the individual investing his or her money has one less thing to worry about.

The 403(b) plans have the same key elements that are characteristic of all annuities: tax deferral, penalties if you make distributions prior to age 59½, and tax-free exchanges. In addition to these standard rules, there are guidelines that employer-sponsored retirement plans must follow. Employers are limited as to how much they can contribute into a plan: 100 percent of an employee's salary or $46,000, whichever is the lesser amount. This stipulation is only for employer-sponsored plans. Remember, in individual annuities, there is not a maximum contribution amount.

With an access code from the nonprofit you work for, you will can open up your annuity online. If your employer does not have an access code, you can go to whoever is in charge of employee benefits. They should be able to give you an enrollment kit.

The TIAA-CREF "Lifecycles" funds allow you to transfer some of the burden of selecting subaccounts over to the insurance company. Rather than trying to select which percentage you want of your premium to go where, the lifecycles funds do this automatically for the investor. You just need to select which year you plan on retiring. Every five years, your account will be rebalanced to meet your changing asset allocation needs.

Things to Consider

- 403(b) plans are the nonprofit sector's alternative to the 401(k) retirement plan. Although 401(k)s are not technically annuities, 403(b)s are and thus are run and managed by insurance companies.

- If your employer matches contributions to your 403(b), you have the added bonus of the extra money from your employer alongside the guarantees that come with annuities making them a potentially superior investment product, even with the maintenance fees associated with tax-sheltered annuities.

Chapter 8

Product Features

Annuities are designed to fulfill a specific function: maximizing your income throughout your retirement and, if desired, for the rest of your life. This is the first and foremost thing you should look for when selecting which product works best for you. Annuities do not have to be just this, however. There are other functions they can fulfill so you may have the retirement you dream of. This chapter will discuss the **riders** you can add to annuities. A rider is a feature of an annuity, or any other insurance product, that is added on to a policy, sometimes for an additional fee. This is an extra of sorts; it is not part of the original policy. Not all riders will be available for all annuities. Insurance companies can customize their products and the corresponding features as long as they conform to their state's insurance laws. For example, you may not find an inflation protection rider and a market value adjustment rider on the same fixed annuity contract. Although there are many choices and many variations of those choices out there, the major riders you should be aware of can be found within this chapter.

Terminal Illness

Many annuity contracts take into account the possibility you could become terminally ill. In this event, if you have a terminal illness rider attached to your annuity, you may be able to make an additional withdrawal from your annuity free of penalty. The percentage available for withdrawal differs from company to company. A doctor's written proof that you are terminally ill is necessary to withdraw money in this manner, as well as some sort of medical record also stating this fact. Some companies set time limits as to how long the annuity, including the rider, has been in effect. For instance, the insurance company might deem that you need to have had the policy for five years prior to utilizing this feature. This rider may come with an additional charge; however, some companies do include it for free.

Long-term Care

If you ever need convalescent care, this rider, or **long-term care insurance**, is a great addition to an annuity. Convalescent care includes stays in skilled nursing facilities or residential care facilities but does not normally include hospital stays. If you are confined to a long-term care facility, you will be able to make an additional withdrawal of a percentage of your annuity without incurring any penalties. This rider may or may not include an additional charge. With new statistics indicating that 50 percent of all individuals will need some sort of convalescent care at some point in their lives, this rider should not be overlooked. Long-term care is expensive. In 2008, the national average cost of stay in an assisted living facility was $3,008 per month, according to the U.S. Department of Health and Human Services at **www.longtermcare.gov**. If you are concerned about preserving assets for your loved ones and do not want to go through the spend-down process associated with Medicaid, long-term care is a matter that needs to be addressed.

Market Value Adjustment

This rider is for fixed annuity accounts for inflation and other ups and downs in the financial markets, including the company's own fluctuating interest rates. If you **liquidate** your annuity early, you may have money added or subtracted to your account, depending on what the market dictates. This is the insurance company's method of protecting its clients and itself from volatile markets. In practice, these accounts will pay higher returns when interest rates go down and a lower set return when the interest rates go up. The value of your account upon withdrawal goes in the opposite direction of the rates offered by the company. This adjustment only occurs when you withdraw funds prematurely, and it is a way for the insurance company to protect its profits. You will most likely pay a penalty if you withdraw funds from these accounts early in addition to any ups or downs the market has posted.

The **market value adjustment** period is the amount of time this rider stays in effect for, lasting up to several years, quite similar to a surrender period. The market value adjustment acts as an incentive to keep your contract in place for the entire term because the insurance company will cut your earnings if you withdraw your money in order to take advantage of better interest rates. This protects the insurance company from clients withdrawing and then reinvesting their funds at higher rates.

The risk in this type of annuity is apparent so why would anyone want to invest in a market value adjustment annuity? Typically, an annuity with this rider will provide a higher rate of return than the average fixed annuity. Only if funds are withdrawn early do the penalties come into play. If the investor is serious about saving for retirement, the guaranteed higher interest rate may be more appealing. You should avoid this feature if you are adverse to risk, however. The market value adjustment feature is only advantageous to the investor if he or she leaves his or her money in the annuity for the entire period that this feature is stipulated for in the contract.

Inflation Adjustment

This is a popular rider with fixed annuities. Inflation protection is attempted by increasing the distribution amount that is received each year. Although the inflation protection helps later on, this rider means the investor will receive less money early on during the annuitization period. Essentially, this rider pays less in the beginning so it can pay you more later. At an average rate of roughly 3 percent each year, inflation is one of the big drawbacks of fixed annuities. This rider, although it does not completely solve the problem, addresses it in a major way.

Another way in which inflation is accounted for is in the allocation of funds. Companies, such as Vanguard, will have holdings in inflation-related products, such as government and corporate bonds. In an investment of this sort, 80 percent of the funds are allocated in such bond instruments, with the remaining 20 percent in noninfla-tion instruments. The noninflation investments are made when bonds rates are low enough to not look attractive to investors, thus keeping the investors' money as competitive as possible.

Income Enhancement

The income enhancement variable annuity rider allows the investor to take more of a gamble with his or her annuity. This rider offers an increase in distribution amounts if bond yields increase to a certain amount over the course of a specified period. Investors who elect to have this rider are gambling on the fact that long-term government bonds will increase their rates during the elected period.

This rider comes at a hefty price; New York Life, for one, charges 3.5 percent of the initial premium. For example, if treasury bond yields rose by only 2 percentage points, monthly distributions may rise from $1,000 to $1,180. Over the course of time, this would greatly outweigh the 3.5 percent fee charged because of the fact that the 3.5 percent fee is usually a one-time payment. Your investment, on the other hand, will grow for years after. If bond yields do not rise, the 3.5 percent charge is simply lost. Unfortunately, most annuity riders do come with such trade-offs. The important thing is that you are comfortable with the fees your annuity charges for the benefits you receive.

Increasing Your Liquidity

Fixed annuities are experiencing an increase in liquid-ity. Because insurance companies want you to keep your money with them, liquidity is always going to be a priority. If you had little or no access to your money when you need it, what would be the incentive for purchasing that product in the first place? Insurance companies are going to continually come up with innovative ideas for increasing your liquidity because of this.

Fixed annuities offer liquidity quite unlike variable annuities. With most variable annuities, the amount available to you changes on a daily basis. Distributions each month will vary with the market conditions your money is exposed to. Because of this, when the market takes a turn for the worse, fixed annuities increase in popularity because they offer a guaranteed return when all other investment vehicles are failing. This has led to the increase in guarantees within variable annuities.

One of the newest riders combines the annuitization lifetime guarantee with an increased liquidity of your account. With this feature, not only are you guaranteed income for life, but you also have ready access to your money. The way it works is quite simple. You annuitize your contract when you are ready to start receiving distributions. At the same time, if you need access to your money, you are able to get some of it readily — without penalty.

This is a new feature, and as such, the kinks are still being worked out. Obviously, if you withdraw too much from your annuity, the lifetime benefits are going to be tiny compared to what you would normally receive. To prevent this from happening, some companies are putting limits as to how much you can withdraw. Regardless, this is a great innovation that definitely merits the attention of potential investors.

Annuity Riders Summary

In a constant struggle to remain competitive, insurance companies will always attempt to advance their products and make them increasingly attractive to prospective clients. Remember though, riders are meant to enhance your investment, not detract from it. Because of this, the cost of any rider you select should be closely examined. If the initial price for the benefit does not give you the value that the actual benefit does, you should rethink the inclusion of it within your annuity contract. The basic premise of an annuity is to preserve your capital for the later years of your retirement. You do not want to throw your money away on expensive riders that do not benefit you in the way they should.

Chapter 9

Subtypes of Annuities

There are hundreds, if not thousands, of variations of annuities so finding the right one might seem like a daunting task. But, there is nothing to fear — there are so many types of annuities out there, the odds of one matching your needs is very high. You just have to know what to look for and where. Do not be confused — subtypes of annuities differ from subaccounts in several different ways. The subaccount of an annuity is the risk class assigned to a portion of a variable annuity. An annuity subtype, on the other hand, is the characteristic that defines what type of annuity the investment actually is and how that annuity functions.

Annuities can be broken up into a few main categories of subtypes:

- When distribution begins

- How you put money into them

- The tax status of the annuity

Determining which categories are best for you is not as difficult as it may seem. The first thing you should look at is the method by which money will be deposited into the account.

Single Premium Annuities

A single premium annuity is merely an annuity purchased with one lump sum of money. The capital can originate from accumulated savings, an inheritance, other investments, or as a rollover from another less competitive annuity or IRA. Fixed annuities are often funded by a single premium. The term "single premium" is sometimes used to describe annuities that are funded with several payments as well, as long as they occur within one year of the contract signing date. After the one-year mark has elapsed, if you want to put more money into a single premium annuity, you will have to sign a new contract. This occurs often; it is not uncommon for an individual to have more than one annuity.

Have you recently received a windfall of money, such as an inheritance? If so, a single premium annuity is an attractive option because you can begin earning interest on the entire amount all at once. Another reason why you may consider a single premium annuity is if you have recently taken a mandatory distribution from an IRA that you do not necessarily need right away. Rather than put the money into a savings account or a CD, it may be more beneficial to take the IRA money and put it into a competitive annuity. Unlike IRA requirements, there is no limit as to how much you can contribute at one time into an annuity. There are also no parameters as to when you must take money out of an annuity, assuming it is not an annuity within an IRA. This aspect of annuities makes them more flexible than an IRA.

Flexible Premium Annuities

A flexible premium annuity is funded by two or more premiums that take place over a period of more than one year. They can be paid for with flexible premiums — where you can alter both the amount you put in each payment and the frequency of payments — or with a scheduled premium — where the amount paid into the annuity is predetermined. Variable annuities often have flexible premiums.

Flexible premium annuities allow you more freedom than other types of annuities. You may vary the amount deposited into the annuity from month to month, even skipping months if you wish. There may be minimum deposits stipulated by the company so make sure you are aware of these prior to skipping payments.

Do you set aside a little bit of money each paycheck for the purpose of investing? In this case, the flexible premium variety will work better for you than a single premium.

One key feature that is unique among flexible variable annuities is **dollar cost averaging**. This method of investing assumes that over the course of time, some shares of the annuity will be bought at low prices and some at higher prices. If done properly over a long enough period, the highs and lows will average out, and the true growth of the account will be profitable. This school of thought assumes that the market has a general upward trend. It also assumes that premiums are paid on a consistent and regular basis, not just when the market is good or when the market is bad.

Good to Know:

This feature works best for individuals who are investing at a younger age and want a long-term investment. Because of dollar cost averaging, these types of annuities will usually grow with the overall market, making the guesswork of when to invest money in regards to market timing less important.

Immediate Annuities

The immediate, or income, annuity refers to the period in which the annuitization period begins in relation to the signing of the contract. Immediate annuities are paid for with a single premium and begin the payout within a year of purchasing. Distributions may be received in a manner that the annuitant deems best; monthly, quarterly, or yearly.

If the immediate annuity has a fixed rate, the amount of each distribution check will be the same. If it is variable, the checks will differ based on your selected portfolio's performance during that particular distribution time and how they affect the overall value of the annuity. Other variables affecting the size of payouts include the amount invested, period selected, and frequency of distributions. The solvency of the insurance company you invest in also determines how much you would receive in distributions because its financial well being dictates the minimum rate. If you need your money soon, an immediate annuity will best serve your needs.

Good to Know:

Immediate annuities are great for people looking for an instant income. Although they do not necessarily provide huge returns, the annuitant will receive a good amount for the remainder of his or her life. Because of increasing life spans, this type of annuity is becoming increasingly popular.

CASE STUDY: RICHARD REYES, THE FINANCIAL QUARTERBACK

Richard Reyes
CFP of Wealth and Business
Planning Group, LLC

Immediate annuities serve a vital purpose, says Richard Reyes, CFP of Wealth and Business Planning Group, LLC. "We specifically only use annuities as a vehicle to prepare for the future distribution of income to maintain a desired standard of living at retirement," Reyes said. "Immediate annuities should always be used as a source from which consistent and predictable income is received."

The way Reyes' firm accomplishes this is rather unique. "A retiree's money is broken up into certain 'buckets of money' with various time frames and different investment vehicles which will allow the client to generate higher returns over time." The approach is rather simple. An immediate variable annuity is put into place to provide for income needs right away while a fixed deferred annuity is also created to provide for needs when the immediate annuity's funds become depleted. Reyes says this approach "will provide for a consistent and predictable income stream for any individual who wants to make sure that he or she never outlives his or her money during retirement." It also avoids any dependence on economic conditions; "Their money is going to grow and be there for them no matter what."

Reyes deals mostly with people in the 'red zone;' people about to retire and people who have just retired. This demographic has needs that others do not. "The planning performed during this time truly defines what success you will have during your retirement years." For one, retirees have more expenses now than they did in the past. Retirees are also living longer than they were in the past. It is crucial that these people have the money supply to support their standard of living during their retirement years.

Reyes, co-author of *The Dirty, Filthy Lies my Broker Taught Me: 101 Truths about Money & Investing*, is also a firm believer that fees and penalties should be kept to a minimum. When using variable annuities, he sticks to the fee only variety where the typical overhead cost of owning the annuity remains extremely low. These policies feature no commission charges, as well as no surrender period — an extremely important feature in case of an emergency. The bulk of those considered for this type of annuity are transferring a nonqualified account from other companies with higher fees. Reyes goes on to comment that, "the financial industry makes tons of money from making the easy complicated. In addition, it makes tons of money from selling product over process." The implication here is that insurance agents will sometimes sell a product that does not fully meet their clients' needs. This is something that Reyes strives to combat.

Deferred Annuities

This type of annuity is for people who do not need the money they are investing for the foreseeable future. Deferred annuities stretch out the period between initial premium and distributions over a period greater than the one-year period of immediate annuities. They can be purchased with single or multiple premiums and both fixed and variable annuities may be deferred. Deferred annuities are best for people who will not need their money returned to them for several years. The most common deferred annuities have surrender periods, where if you need to access your money early by annuitization, you can, but you will have to pay a penalty. These penalties will start out around 10 percent and diminish as time goes on, around the rate of 1 percent per year.

Good to Know:

This type of annuity works well with people who do not necessarily need all of their savings in the near future. Deferred annuities make for a great long-term investment because they accumulate interest over a larger portion of your money than the same amount invested in an immediate annuity.

Bonus Annuities

This type of annuity offers an additional rate of return for at least the first year of the contract. This is meant to attract eager clients with a high interest rate guaranteed for the first year, while subsequent years might not be as beneficial to the annuitant. The **bonus** may or may not be available beyond the first year so when looking at this type of annuity, make sure to examine whether a lower rate in the later years is something you are willing to accept. Bonus annuity contracts must be reviewed carefully because of this.

Some bonus annuities will add a certain percentage of your investment to the initial premium, some as high as 10 percent. With this type of annuity, a $100,000 premium would start out as $110,000. Generally speaking though, the larger the bonus, the longer the surrender period will be. Insurance companies want to make sure they recover the amount of money they give away, and this can only be accomplished if their investments stay within the company.

When dealing with transferring money from one annuity to another with a bonus rate, always remember that you will be subject to a new surrender charge — if you withdraw money early, you may be forfeiting the bonus that enticed you to sign the policy in the first place.

Good to Know:

Bonus annuities are a great way to earn "free money." But, be careful, enticing bonuses often come with higher rates and longer surrender periods. If you decide the annuity is still worthwhile despite these stipulations, then a bonus annuity can help you greatly.

Qualified Annuities

A qualified annuity is an annuity bought with money that has not yet been taxed. These can consist of IRA and Roth IRA annuities, as well as 403(b) plans. The benefit to these annuities is, once again, their tax deferral. Qualified annuities are taxed later in life, normally when the annuitant is retired and in a lower tax bracket. This makes the tax burden a bit lighter than if the annuitant was to simply put his or her money in a mutual fund or a CD where funds are subject to capital gains taxes each year. It also allows the money that would normally be taxed to gain interest for the annuitant, resulting in even higher gains.

Nonqualified Annuities

A nonqualified annuity is an annuity bought with money that has previously been taxed. Although increases in the annuity will be taxed as income under the tax bracket that the annuitant falls under at the time of distribution, the principal amount, because it has already been taxed once, will not be taxed again, leaving only the profits to be taxed at the rate determined by the exclusion ratio. You can use the chart on the following page to compare the advantages and disadvantages of each type of annuity.

TYPE OF ANNUITY	ADVANTAGES	DISADVANTAGES
Qualified	Lightens immediate tax load	May push investor into a higher tax bracket upon annuitization
Nonqualified	Will not be taxed twice and not subject to deposit restrictions	Pre-tax dollars cannot be used
Immediate	Offers immediate access to annuity funds	Funds do not accumulate as much interest as deferred annuities
Deferred	Funds accumulate more interest time than immediate annuities	Subject to surrender periods if annuitization is selected
Single Premium	Allows for a large investment that cannot be achieved with IRAs	Only premiums paid within the first year may be used
Flexible Premium	Dollar cost averaging	Interest rates may change for the worse over time

Chapter 10

Annuity Options

Annuities can be extremely versatile investment vehicles. Almost any feature from other types of investments can be incorporated into an annuity. This only makes them more attractive to investors who know what they are looking for. There are so many options out there, however, that it makes annuities seem much more confusing than they need to be. With a bit of understanding, you will know exactly what it is you are looking for and select the corresponding annuity. There are literally thousands of annuities in the U.S. to choose from so why not select the one that best fits the needs you have rather than the one an insurance agent tries to sell you.

Annuities and IRAs

Annuities can act as a home for other investment products, such as an IRA. To fully comprehend this, think of the annuity as a van, with the IRA as the driver. The IRA is still subject to all the laws and regulations that cover an IRA, but the annuity conforms to the laws that govern other annuities, just as a van would be subject to traffic laws while the driver of the van is subject to the laws of citizens, too.

Both IRAs and Roth IRAs are valuable retirement tools, and you may want to consider housing them in an annuity. But, remember that with IRAs, you are subject to the yearly maximum contribution limit, and with Roth IRAs, you are still subject to the maximum yearly salary caps. Also, IRAs can only receive contributions that are earned. Capital gains earnings cannot be used to fund IRAs or Roth IRAs. Although the annuity does offer an added degree of protection, investors are still subject to all IRA regulations.

The purchase of an annuity may help an investor convert some of his or her excess earnings to a Roth IRA. Mutual fund income may push taxable earnings per year above the Roth IRA earnings threshold, especially if the mutual fund has a good year. For Roth IRAs, there is currently a $105,000 annual income limit for individuals wishing to make a full contribution. This amount may change slightly each year to account for inflation and the national average earnings rate so be sure to check the current earnings threshold before you invest. Additionally, partial contributions may be made for those earning no more than $120,000. Income from a mutual fund may affect the account owner in a way that causes ineligibility for a Roth IRA if that investor is near the yearly earnings limit.

Here is an example: Consider Anne, a single woman who earns $90,000 per year through her employer. Anne has a portfolio of mutual funds worth $300,000. If the mutual funds gain 10 percent over the course of the year ($30,000), it will push her yearly income up to $120,000, thus making her ineligible to invest any of her money in a Roth IRA.

If Anne had her $300,000 in a variable annuity that produced the same 10 percent rate of return, because that money grows tax-deferred, she would still be eligible to apply for a Roth IRA. The $30,000 gained would remain in the annuity until she withdraws it during retirement, and it would not be classified as income. Only when the annuitization period began would the annuity be taxed. At that point, the need for a Roth IRA will have passed.

Roth IRAs, although more restrictive as to who can own them, are much more appealing because of their tax benefits. Return to Anne, a hypothetical example, for a more in depth look at this.

Anne has finally purchased an IRA. At age 40, she still has quite a bit of time before retirement, and she plans on contributing $3,000 per year up to age 65, for a total contribution of $75,000. Her IRA at age 65 would be worth $357,049 with a consistent 10 percent interest rate. At the 15 percent tax bracket, she would have to pay about $53,557 in taxes. If she had fallen within the earnings guidelines and purchased a more restrictive Roth IRA, with all other conditions being the same, she would have the same $357,049 tax-free upon reaching age 65.

As a point of comparison, take a look at what would have happened had Anne bought a 10 percent guaranteed fixed annuity under the exact same conditions. Again, $75,000 would be invested, with $282,049 being taxable, which at 15 percent comes to $42,307 payable to Uncle Sam. But, rather than having to pay all $42,307 of her taxes at once, she would only pay the taxes at the exclusion ratio upon the withdrawal of her money. The longer she kept the money in the annuity, the less she would be paying in taxes, and with annuities, there is no mandatory withdrawal age as there is with IRAs.

Annuities as a CD

A fairly recent addition to the world of annuities are those that act like certificates of deposit. These are fixed annuities that are meant to mimic CDs. **CD-type annuities** offer more competitive rates than CDs, but they do have downfalls. For one, it is more expensive than usual to break the annuity contract and withdraw your money early. CD-type annuities last between five and ten years and have stiff penalties if you need your money before that period is up. They also are not FDIC insured as CDs are. This fact gives them a slight element of risk that CDs do not have. The CD-type annuities are still subject to the same laws as annuities — if the investor withdraws the money before age 59½, there is still and 10 percent IRS penalty. CDs have no age restrictions when it comes to receiving funds.

There are advantages to CD-type annuities over CDs, though. For one, annuities are still tax-deferred. CDs are not; the investor must pay yearly capital gains on the profits from a CD. Also, as mentioned before, CD-type annuities offer better rates, normally a full percentage point higher than their CD brethren.

There are also CD-type annuities with contracts for as little as one year. With a one-year surrender period, this investment acts just like a 12-month CD. If you are in the beginning years of your retirement, this product becomes useful when you are shopping around for just the right investment. These are also useful if interest rates for multi-year agreements are low. Rather than lock your money up in a complicated and not very profitable investment, you will have access to your money in just one year, while earning a higher rate of return in the process. This allows you to transfer your investment to a product with a higher rate of return without incurring a penalty and earn interest in the interim.

Income Annuities

Income annuities, also known as **immediate annuities**, were briefly touched upon in Chapter 9. They are designed to fulfill the same function as a company pension would: They offer you immediate money you can live off during your retirement years. Income annuities are a type of immediate annuity, meaning that when you put money into them, you see payouts in less than one year. These provide a good opportunity for the retiree to convert his or her savings into a flow of income. The period this stream of income lasts for is determined between the investor and the insurance company, but some companies allow you to choose a straight life option and receive income for life, no matter how long that might be.

Some professionals advise that as a general rule, you should never place more than 30 percent of your assets into an income annuity. Although you will be receiving your money back in a very short time, you do not want to freeze money you may need for emergencies or unexpected expenses. Some experts argue that if you need the money, you can place up to 100 percent of your savings into an income annuity. This will certainly give you the biggest profits. But, this is not practical because you will have to pay a hefty penalty if for some reason you do need the money sooner than expected.

Variable income annuities have a few added benefits. Besides the potential for guaranteed income for life, they have inflation protection because they are directly related to an index or group of stocks. This gives you the most amount of freedom with your investment because you can allocate your own assets in the manner that best suits your needs. If this degree of freedom is not necessary and you are worried about downtrends in the market, it is always possible to put a portion of your assets in a variable income annuity and another portion into a fixed income annuity.

With variable income annuities, the investor is responsible for choosing an **assumed interest rate**. This rate is how your first distributions will be determined. Many experts recommend being pessimistic in this decision by choosing a low interest rate. This serves a couple purposes, the first being it gives you a realistic look at the minimum you will probably be receiving over the course of the contract. Also, if you aim low, it is always nice to be pleasantly surprised with extra money later in the payout period. By aiming low, you ensure that if the market performs well, you will receive more money during the latter part of your retirement.

Choosing the wrong assumed interest rate is not a catastrophe for those who live longer because everything will even out over time. Short-term results will vary, however. Choosing a high assumed interest rate will give you smaller distributions during the later years of your retirement if the market sours. The opposite is also true; a lower elected assumed interest rate will give you larger distributions.

One piece of information that must be acknowledged is that if an investor lives long enough, his or her entire annuity distribution would become taxable at the rate determined by the investor's income tax bracket. The **exclusion ratio** proclaims that annuities are taxed on a last-in, first-out basis. Once the exclusion ratio determines that the original investment has been distributed, it would reach zero, and the investor would be responsible to pay full income taxes on the amount received.

Advanced Life Deferred Annuities

Advanced Life Deferred Annuities, also called longevity insurance annuities, are a rather uncommon type of annuity, but they do warrant at least a mention. Resembling insurance more than an investment, ALDAs only pay out if you live to a certain age, normally 80. If the investor passes away prior to that age, there is no pay out. Once the investor reaches the chosen age, the annuitization phase begins with a much more generous payout than a regular annuity would have because the estimated lifespan of the investor is much shorter.

This may seem unattractive, and to most people it is. But, there are some advantages to an ALDA. They address the issue of outliving your money. In your later years, there is absolutely no risk of running out of money, and the payouts you receive will be greater than a payout from the average deferred annuity. Because of this, **expense planning** is made much easier. You do not have to worry about spending too much during the earlier years of your retirement because you will be compensated throughout your later years.

With ALDAs, you do have other options. Although the cheapest ALDA has no cash value redeemable upon death, there are more attractive choices out there. You can en-roll in a joint-survivor account, which pays as long as one spouse is still alive. There are also cash refunds available with some ALDAs, which will redeem any unpaid premi-ums to a beneficiary as long as both spouses die prior to receiving their initial payment. A final choice offered by some companies is a death benefit, which would be pay-able to beneficiaries.

Annuities as a Tool

Most individuals use annuities as a tool for accomplish-ing a goal. There are many risks and factors that affect a retiree, including the death of a spouse or other loved one, outliving savings, placement in a nursing home, inflation, and other emergencies. Annuities can handle all of these risks if used correctly.

If you have ever had to transfer a loved one to a nursing home, you know how expensive this can be. An annuity with a convalescent care rider would help minimize these costs. This option would allow the annuitant to withdraw an extra percentage from his or her annuity without incur-ring any penalty.

Annuities can also cover the positive aspects of retirement, such as traveling, moving, or just living comfortably. De-pending on your goals and situation, annuities can be a useful tool.

Chapter 11

Customizing your Annuity

By now, you should have a clear understanding regarding the basic purposes and options that come along with owning an annuity. Now, it is time to talk about investing strategies. You should view all annuities as a way to reduce stress and financial hardship during your retirement, but this chapter will talk about the specifics that the investor should look for to maximize these goals. With the right kind of investing, you can get the maximum return on your money while minimizing your risk of loss and exposure to any penalties you might face.

Staging your Investments

Some researchers argue that you should not part with all of the money you wish to invest all at once. This is for two reasons: One, it allows you to keep more money earlier in your retirement for unexpected costs, and two, it gives you the option of investing in cheaper products with higher interest rates as you grow older.

As you age, you will want to transfer money from higher risk products to lower risk products. So, a man at age 30 will want to have less money in annuities than a man at age 65. If a variable annuity is bought at age 30, the investor will want to have money in other higher-risk investment products as well. Once he gets closer to retirement, his needs will change and other more conservative annuities should be purchased in order to compensate for this.

Staging can be done with both variable and fixed annuities. Using fixed annuities to create a string of investments is a common practice among annuity investors. Rather than investing a lump sum into one annuity, the investor spreads out investments with the hopes that the rate of return will increase as time goes by. This makes sure all of your investing money is not locked into a low rate. Investors also will want to spread out maturity dates so their investments are not due back to them all at the same time. For example, buying a set of fixed deferred annuities that mature in five, seven, ten, and 12 years will not only spread out when you start receiving your distributions, but it will also set up a defense against inflation. This is done by rolling over the lower-rate annuities when they mature into an annuity with higher, inflation-combating rates.

Social Security

The earliest you can begin receiving traditional **Social Security** benefits is at age 62. There is a downfall to receiving your benefits early though — you will not receive as much per month. Many people wish to wait until they reach age 70, the age at which Social Security distributions become mandatory, because the amount they will receive is currently more than 50 percent higher. Think of Social Security acting as an annuity does; you will receive distributions per month the longer you wait to accept it because you will, in theory, have a shorter remaining lifespan than someone five years younger.

If you are in the camp of people who wish to wait until later so they can have the higher amount from the government each month, an immediate income annuity may be right for you because it can supplement your income during the years you go without Social Security. Rather than accepting Social Security at age 62, you could purchase an immediate annuity with your savings. This way, you will have a source of income while you wait for the higher rate from your Social Security check.

Split annuities

This is a common practice among savvy investors. A **split annuity** refers to the practice of dividing money between two annuity accounts: one deferred and one immediate. The immediate annuity should get about 40 percent of the amount planned for investing, with the remaining 60 percent going into a deferred account. With the immediate annuity, the investor has money to live off right away, while the deferred annuity creates a nest egg that will benefit him or her further down the road.

Fixed or variable annuities can be used in this fashion; it does not matter which you choose to use. The only caveat is that the deferred annuity must be allowed to grow until it equals the original amount invested. Once this occurs, the process is repeated. The deferred annuity is liquidated and immediately invested in the two annuities in the same manner as before.

For example, assume $1,000,000 was invested in this manner. So, $600,000 would be placed in a deferred account, while $400,000 was placed in an immediate account. The $400,000 plus the interest it gains would be enough to support a family while the deferred annuity sat and grew. If the deferred annuity grew at a rate of 10 percent per year, after seven years, the deferred account would equal $1,062,936.60. The deferred annuity would be cashed out once the surrender period was over so the process could then be repeated after this point; $400,000 placed in an immediate annuity and the rest into a deferred one.

As you can see, this method is most effective with large amounts of money. If the same exercise was tried with $100,000, the family would have only the $40,000 plus interest to live on for the seven years before their deferred annuity had grown large enough to repeat the cycle. As a standalone investment, this would not be feasible, but when you take into account other investments, such as company pensions, IRAs, and Social Security benefits, this strategy is made much more accessible to the average investor.

This strategy is also most effective with annuities containing shorter surrender periods. There is little use in cashing out your holdings if you are then hit with an 8 percent penalty for accessing your money too early.

Home equity

It is possible to turn the equity in your home to income with an annuity. This is popular among investors who have not saved enough for retirement and find themselves scrambling for another source of income once they reach retirement age. A **home equity conversion mortgage**, also known as a **reverse mortgage**, allows you to retain ownership of your home. It is a loan based on your home's value, interest rates, and your life expectancy. If you find you have simply not saved enough for retirement, this may be your best option.

There are a few options with this type of transaction. You can receive the money borrowed all at once, as a line of credit, or as monthly distributions. The money borrowed can then be invested into an annuity, hopefully at a better interest rate than what your mortgage payment was, thus giving you a slight profit. The borrowed money can be converted to income, some of which will probably be used to repay the reverse mortgage loan payments.

There are expenses associated with reverse mortgages so they are not in everyone's best interest. Although it will be necessary over time for you or your heirs to repay the loan, it can offer a quick fix to investors feeling the pinch of not having enough money. Reverse mortgages do not need to be repaid as long as one homeowner is living. After the death of all homeowners, beneficiaries may choose to convert the reverse mortgage into a normal mortgage or sell the home in order to repay the amount borrowed. Rates for reverse mortgages are normally higher than traditional mortgages.

A portfolio of annuities

As an investor gets closer to retirement, annuities increase in attractiveness. This is because annuities can provide a guarantee like few other investments. You are promised that there will be money available each month for the rest of your life when it is needed. Transferring other types of investments to annuities will become more beneficial to the annuitant as they age, and their portfolio allocation becomes more conservative. A need for more than one annuity contract may emerge as a result.

With the right blending of fixed, equity-indexed, and variable annuities, not only does the investor provide for themselves during retirement, but it also is possible to prepare for final expenses. Of course, the investor must always be aware of the degree of risk he or she is willing to take. A conservative investor will want the vast majority of his or her annuity money in a fixed account, while the more aggressive investor should purchase a variable annuity. The variable annuity will take care of keeping up with inflation, and the fixed annuity provides a guaranteed income for life. An immediate income annuity provides income right away, and an advanced life deferred annuity will provide extra income for later years; this is especially useful if the investor or a loved one needs custodial care or in the event that previous investments lose value because of failing markets. Having more than one annuity in your portfolio can then provide for a multitude of needs.

If each separate contract of your portfolio of annuities is purchased at different times, the usefulness of your money is increased because you have more access to funds when you will need it during your early retirement years. For example, an investor should have a higher-risk variable annuity during the years approaching retirement. Shortly after retirement, an income annuity could be purchased in order to supplement the soon-to-come Social Security benefits. Then, after ten years or so, an advanced life deferred annuity could be purchased to combat the cost of a potential stay at a nursing home and final expenses because of the higher earnings advanced life deferred annuities pay out.

A variable annuity bought early on in one's life can have enormous potential. The great thing about these market-dependent investments is that they can be remolded to fit any life needs. To readjust assets, the investor need only make a phone call to his or her agent.

Whether you choose to invest in fixed or variable annuities, a portfolio of annuities can be a great help. As inflation occurs, fixed annuities will be forced to increase their rates in order to stay relevant while variable annuities naturally keep up with inflation. Either way, the investor benefits.

Annuities within a Portfolio

Annuities do not necessarily need to cover all of your bases as an investor. An annuity can easily be one part of a well-rounded portfolio. When placed alongside mutual funds, life insurance, stock and bond holdings, IRAs, and Treasury Notes, annuities fulfill functions that none of these other investments do: a way to grow your money on a tax-deferred basis, and a way to give you a guaranteed income for life.

In fact, by using an annuity as simply one piece of a greater puzzle, you can reduce the risk of inflicting a penalty upon yourself if you need direct access to money. With money in cash accounts and penalty-free investments, the odds that you will have to break into your annuity prior to the end of the surrender period are greatly reduced. If tragedy does occur and you are forced to dissipate your money quickly because of unforeseen circumstances, the annuity will still be there as a safety net for the rest of your life.

Chapter 12

Tax Specifications and Other Penalties

he tax laws concerning annuities are abundant and confusing. Because annuities are such a complex product, they can
be very confusing to the average investor. There are early withdrawal penalties and IRS Section 1035 exchanges, for one. Not
every company charges all of these fees, though, so shop around
to avoid some of them. But, be aware that if there is not a fee for
a particular service, it may be because that service is not included
with the annuity contract. If you feel that a particular service is
necessary for you, make sure it is included in your contract.

The Basics About Taxation

Annuities grow tax-deferred, meaning, they are not taxed until
the money is withdrawn. This differentiates them from CDs,
money market accounts, and stocks and bonds, which are taxable
at the end of each fiscal year This severely limits the growth of
these non-tax-deferred investments because the full amount does
not gain interest. But, because annuities are tax-deferred, they
avoid this, allowing interest to compound. Interest is paid on the
principal, past interest earnings, and tax savings.

When the annuitization period begins on a nonqualified annuity, the money that was put in last is taxed first. This process is referred to as last in, first out, or LIFO. The reasoning for this is that earned interest is added to accounts last. Face it — the IRS gets what belongs to them. Because they have already taken a share out of the principal, only the interest remains to be taxed. Seen in this light, the LIFO process makes much more sense. If the annuity was purchased prior to 1981, however, annuitants can withdraw on a first-in, first-out basis. With annuities purchased prior to 1981, annuitants receive their principal and deposits back first; because there is no interest received by the annuitant, he or she pays no taxes. But, because growth and income are taken out of the annuity first on the newer LIFO annuities, you will pay more taxes on your first withdrawals than you will on later withdrawals.

Qualified accounts are 100 percent subject to income taxes because qualified money has not been taxed prior to investing it. You will pay Uncle Sam his due at some point, whether it is now or later, qualified or nonqualified. Remember though, if you have a qualified account, the amount that would normally be taxed will be working for you rather than being taken away.

Because annuities grow tax-deferred, they have a distinct advantage over other investment products. One of the most commonly used alternatives to annuities is the mutual fund. Mutual funds are taxed each year, causing a severe lack in capital accumulation.

Take a look at the following chart to see how a $10,000 initial premium would act in both a tax-deferred account and in a taxable account:

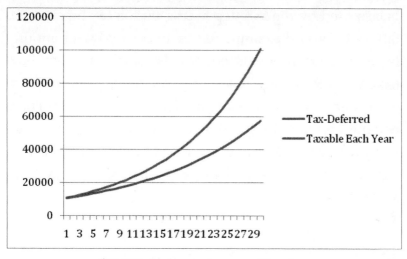

$10,000 single premium annuities at an
8 percent interest rate over 30 years.

As you can see, the tax-deferred account grows to more than $100,000 over the course of 30 years. The taxable account is more than $40,000 less over the same period.

To calculate your own chart, you will need a few key pieces of data. You will need to know how much you use as an initial deposit, whether you will make consistent additions to the annuity, and if yes, how much those premiums will be. You will also have to make a few assumptions. What interest rate do you think you will get on your investment? How long will you keep your money within the annuity prior to taking distributions? The chart used here assumes an 8 percent interest rate.

Early withdrawal

The IRS invokes a 10 percent penalty if you withdraw money from an annuity prior to the age of 59½, unless you become permanently disabled and are able to provide the proper documentation. The interest earned will be assessed by the IRS depending on the tax bracket you fall under, and the company you purchased your annuity from will also apply surrender fees contingent upon how long you have held the annuity. As mentioned previously, annuities are designed to aid in your retirement. These penalties were put into place to encourage this and avoid inappropriate use of annuities, such as **money laundering**, a way of concealing illegally obtained money from authorities.

Surrender fees

When discussing options with an insurance salesman, be sure to ask about the surrender fees associated with the product you are considering. Some surrender charges can be as high as 15 percent. If you fall ill and need the money sooner, you want to make sure there are options for you. Ask whether it is possible to have surrender fees waived altogether in the event of a terminal illness, as this rider can sometimes be added to annuity contracts for an additional fee.

Surrender fees often decline as the contract ages. For example, the contract may call for an 8-percent charge against your account if you withdraw more than 10 percent during the second year but only charge you 2 percent if you withdraw the same percentage during the eighth year. The following chart illustrates what a typical surrender fee schedule might look like.

Year of contract	1	2	3	4	5	6	7	8	9	10
Penalty	10%	8%	7%	6%	5%	4%	3%	2%	1%	0%

Contract fees

This is a fee associated with the paperwork and processing of your contract. Contract fees may come as a one-time charge or annually as you renew your contract. Some companies, such as Vanguard, do not charge contract fees.

Transaction fees

This is a fee the insurance company might deduct from your annuity with each premium payment you provide. It may come as a flat rate or as a percentage of the premium. Most companies do not charge this fee.

The tier system

Annuities come either as single tiered or two tiered, with single-tiered annuities being much more common. With this method, once the surrender period is over, the annuitant can withdraw all of his or her money without incurring a penalty. Two-tiered annuities offer higher rates of return, but in exchange, you give up some freedom. With this type of contract, annuitants must annuitize their investment, meaning they can never have access to all of their money unless they pay a hefty fee.

Premium taxes

In some states, there is a tax levied on premiums. The company may deduct this at the time of each premium payment, upon withdrawals, or when it pays a death benefit to your beneficiary. To find out more about whether your state has such a tax law, consult an accountant or tax specialist, or visit **www.gilico.com/premiumtaxes.html**.

Internal Revenue Code Section 1035

Section 1035 of the IRS code refers to the laws that regulate exchanges between insurance products. Among other things, the law prohibits selling annuities for the sake of commission alone. The insurance agent must spell out the positive and negative aspects of any exchange so the client has a full understanding of what he or she is doing. These laws were put in place to prevent salesmen from abusing annuity and insurance sales simply to gain a commission. Information must be strictly spelled out so the client making the exchange benefits from the deal.

These 1035 exchanges are simple on the behalf of the annuity owner. Only a couple forms need to be filled out; you do not even need to contact your old company if you are switching from one to another. The insurance company you are switching over to will provide everything you need. This process can be very slow, though. There is paperwork that each company needs to fill out and certain time frames that it must be completed in. This inevitably slows down the process of an exchange.

Another key feature of 1035 exchanges is that taxes do not have to be paid out during the exchange. There are no withholdings processed when one account is closed and the other is opened. You will not pay taxes on your annuity until you or your heir personally starts receiving distributions from it.

You can exchange annuities for a few reasons, with one being better rates. If one company offers a product with superior returns to another, you are allowed to exchange. Another reason to exchange is the quality of service. For instance, if one company refuses to meet with you face to face and another always sends an agent to your home when you have questions, this may be a simple enough reason to exchange. You cannot exchange policies simply because you like one agent better than another or because the agent offered you some sort of reward for signing up. This practice, known as rebating, is forbidden under most states' insurance laws if the gift given is done based solely upon your enrollment in a policy.

Life insurance policies can be transferred to an annuity through Section 1035 if for some reason you find your needs change. For example, assume you have a life insurance policy that was meant to pay off your mortgage. If you have finished paying this debt off, you may want to rethink your goals with the money you have invested in that life insurance policy and switch over to an annuity. With whole life insurance policies, the entire amount of money invested can be transferred into an annuity rather than surrendering the whole life policy for its cash value. A whole life policy's cash value, which is oftentimes borrowed by policyholders, is much less than the amount invested into the policy.

Annuities cannot be transferred into a life insurance policy with 1035 exchanges. This is because your annuity cash sum is money designated for your own personal use. Life insurance is not intended for the insured's use; it is designed for your heirs to use in order to pay final expenses. Life insurance cash values can, however, be converted to an annuity. The reasoning for this is the fact that you can use your insurance cash value at any time. You can even borrow from it without facing tax repercussions. If you have not repaid it at the time of your death, the amount borrowed is simply taken out of the death benefit your heir would normally receive.

One final note on 1035 exchanges is that an exchanged contract will start at the beginning of the surrender period for the new contract. If, after five years, you exchange your old annuity contract for a new one with a seven-year surrender period, you must wait the entire seven years before you can surrender your annuity penalty-free. There is no carryover of time from contract to contract.

For more information on 1035 exchanges, visit **www.immediateannuities.com/library_articles/section_1035_exchange.htm**.

Internal Revenue Code Section 408

The IRS states that annuities may be used to fund traditional and Roth IRAs. For all intents and purposes, an annuity that fell under this heading would act just like an IRA or Roth IRA. There would still be the contribution limits, earning limits, and timeframes that characterize IRAs. But, the earnings would be determined by the annuity part of it.

Returning to the van metaphor used in an earlier chapter, the IRA is the driver of the van and is subject to all laws it would normally be subject to as the driver and as a citizen. Laws and regulations that apply to both annuities and IRAs must be followed, such as the minimum age for penalty-free withdrawals. This means that although the IRA is subject to IRA laws and regulations, the complete package, when it comes time to determine how earnings are accredited, is determined as if it were an annuity. In other words, the IRA would be handled like an annuity, yet still fall under IRA laws.

The annuity, as the van, is still subject to independent annuity regulations including the stipulation that they can only be sold by insurance agents or agencies.

Exclusion ratio

The **exclusion ratio** is the formula that determines what amount of your annuity is taxable and what will be returned to you tax-free. It should be noted that this is only relevant to nonqualified annuities, or annuities purchased with money that has already been taxed. Qualified annuities are completely subject to taxation because you have not yet paid taxes on them.

Your investment's profits will be taxed in a nonqualified account, but the principal will be received tax-free because you have already paid taxes on it. Many factors come into play when determining the exclusion ratio, including the principal amount, the amount of each distribution, and the number of years you are expected to live, calculated by a mortality table. The formula for determining the taxable rate is complicated, but luckily, it is calculated by your insurance company. The IRS's mortality table can be found **www.irs.gov/irb/2007-09_IRB/ar07.html**.

A simple way to approximate your exclusion ratio is to take the ending amount of your investment and divide it by the principal. For instance, if your annuity is now worth $200,000, and you paid $100,000 into it throughout the life of the contract, your exclusion ratio is 50 percent. So, if you are receiving distributions of $8,000, roughly half of that — $4,000 — is subject to taxation. This allows you to pay a smaller amount of taxes with each withdrawal rather than worrying about paying a large lump sum all at once.

Beneficiaries and taxes

The tax burden placed upon a beneficiary is a bit more complicated. In short, beneficiaries only pay income taxes on the earnings of the annuity that is passed down to them, even though the entire annuity is income to them. This is the case if they decide to take the annuity payout in one lump sum. If he or she chooses to, the beneficiary can also convert the annuity to a monthly benefit. An individual may choose to do this if the annuitization of the contract would be beneficial to him or her in some way. It would also lower the immediate tax burden.

Another option involves letting the contract sit for up to five years. Legally, five years is the longest the beneficiary can wait before accepting the annuity as a lump sum. The annuity would continue to earn interest for the five-year period. If need be, the beneficiary can make withdrawals or transfer money between subaccounts of the annuities. Any extra income more than the post-tax dollar premiums will be taxable when the withdrawals are made.

If the beneficiary is the spouse of the annuitant, there is another option available. The spouse may choose to take over the annuity as owner. If this occurs, all rights of the annuity are transferred to the survivor. The annuity can be held or annuitized as it would have been if the original owner was still living. Taxes would be due at the time of withdrawal, if and when that takes place.

If the original annuity owner is concerned about the tax status of his or her heirs, there is a preventative measure that can be taken. Advising heirs to withdraw smaller amounts, so as not to incur a large income tax spike, is the best way to avoid losses because of tax.

Annuities and Your Taxes

As long as your money is in the tax-deferred account, you do not need to claim the earnings your money may see on your income tax report. If you withdraw money from the annuity or annuitize the contract, it then becomes fair game for the IRS because the money will then be taxed. If you do your own taxes, you need to be aware of which tax bracket you are in, and whether or not the income from your annuity, as determined by the exclusion ratio, will push you into a higher bracket.

Avoiding taxes legally

Who does not want to preserve their assets? Although it is impossible to avoid taxes completely, there are a few tips that will allow you to minimize the amount you give to the government.

You can elect to have smaller distributions, or annuitize over a longer period. The less money withdrawn at one time, the less likely you are to be bumped up into the next tax bracket. The less money you take in over the course of a year, the lower your taxes will be.

Tax exemptions can also be preserved through the ownership of annuities. If a family's income is artificially made too high by income from a mutual fund, they will be pushed into a higher tax bracket. Owning an annuity would keep the family inside the tax bracket they earn solely through their labor. The increase in income taxes that a successful mutual fund portfolio would create can be avoided with a variable annuity invested in the same manner. Again, this is thanks to the tax-deferral benefit of annuities.

Purchasing a Roth IRA inside of an annuity is also a way to avoid paying taxes. The biggest stipulation here is that Roth IRAs must be bought with income from an employer. It is illegal to purchase a Roth IRA with income from other assets. Using profits from a mutual fund or stock market investment would fall under this category. Starting in 2010, there are no earning caps on the conversion of a traditional IRA to a Roth IRA.

If you are still concerned about taxation, consider consulting a tax professional with experience regarding annuities and their tax benefits.

Capital gains

Annuity profits are not subject to **capital gains** taxes like a mutual fund would be. Profits are taxed merely as income. You will still need to file a separate form when it comes time to file your taxes. The 1099-R form is discussed soon.

The downside to this is that annuity income is generally taxed at a higher rate, depending on your tax bracket. Capital gains, the tax code for profits from stock market related products, are currently taxed at 15 percent, a rate lower than the nation's average tax bracket. This rate stays the same regardless of which tax bracket you belong to. The saving grace to annuity proceeds being taxed as income rather than capital gains is that retirees normally fall into a lower tax bracket once they stop receiving income from their place of employment and begin receiving social security. The tax brackets for 2010 are stipulated in the chart below.

2010 Single Tax Filers	Rate of Taxation	Capital Gains
Income Range		
$0-$8,375	10%	20%
$8,375.01-$34,000	15%	20%
$34,000.01-$82,400	25%	20%
$82,400.01-$171,850	28%	20%
$171,850.01-$373,650	33%	20%
$373,650.01 and up	35%	20%

Under current income tax laws, the upper bracket of taxpayers is charged 35 percent of their income. This is only for people making $373,650.01 or more per year for 2010. The capital gains rate for these individuals is 20 percent lower and would be more advantageous. This is one of the biggest downfalls involving annuities. It is also the main factor that keeps the wealthy out of the annuity market.

College savings

Under current tax laws, it is possible to set aside money in an annuity and not declare it as savings when applying for financial aid. The college loan application process has become very strict over the years, and this is a completely legal way to help your child have easier access to financial aid. The Free Application for Federal Student Aid (FAFSA) form for the 2009-2010 school year specifically states that assets held in annuities do not need to be stated when applying for financial aid. This makes annuities a great tool for helping your children receive government loans. Mutual funds, on the other hand, must be reported. Because of the fact that annuities are mainly used as retirement vessels and mutual funds have multiple uses, the government views the two different products differently.

The 1099-R form

The 1099-R tax form is what indicates to the IRS that annuity funds have been received by an individual. These will be sent out by the insurance company in order to show the IRS that annuity funds have been paid out. Whenever you receive money from an annuity or complete a 1035 exchange, you will receive the 1099-R form. There are several variations of the 1099, but for most intents and purposes regarding annuities, the 1099-R form will be the only one you must become familiar with.

I need my money early — now what?

If an emergency does arise and you need your money early, there are ways to get out of annuities early. You have probably seen the advertisements on television where companies offer to buy your annuity from you. Although it is not always easy to access your money early, it is possible. Insurance companies do understand that emergencies arise. This is why you can withdraw 10 percent of your annuity penalty-free each year prior to the annuitization of your contract. Besides these systematic withdrawals, there are a few other methods of accessing your money. If 10 percent of your investment is not enough to meet your needs, there are other ways to access your money. Each of these methods are laid out in detail below.

Selling Annuities: You can sell an annuity prior to the end of the annuitization period — but it will cost you. Say you have invested $100,000 in an annuity and have just started your payout phase. You are receiving $1,500 each month and have 100 distributions payments remaining, for a total of $150,000 dollars. However, your annuity is currently only worth $120,000 because the full term of the annuity has not been reached. An outside company may agree to purchase your annuity for $110,000. Although these are just examples, you will notice you do pay a hefty price for selling your annuity early.

It should be noted that not all annuities can be sold in this manner. The annuity in question must be nonqualified and cannot be a straight life product. This is a way to access your money if you need a large sum of cash quickly.

Getting Out of Your Contract: This question must be addressed on an individual basis. It is true that most annuities can be sold, but it differs from company to company. You can do so by either selling all or part of your annuity to an outside company. The amount you receive, as seen in the previous example, will not be the same as what you were expecting to receive if you held onto the annuity indefinitely. The annuity buyer would then hold on to your contract until the term is complete or resell it at a profit.

Converting Your Annuity: Again, with most annuities you can convert to a lump sum of cash, while others will not allow you to do this. The process takes anywhere from a few weeks to a few months depending on your annuity's contract and the company you are dealing with. Most companies understand that emergencies do arise and try to be accommodating. But, this is an instance in which a surrender period would apply if your annuity was liquidated early.

Annuitizing Early: This option exists for almost every type of annuity out there, even deferred annuities. If you have bought a deferred annuity and need the cash quick, most companies will allow you to annuitize the contract, even if less than a year has gone by. This is an instance where your deferred annuity can become an immediate annuity. Some companies may charge a small fee if you annuitize too early, but if you need the money early, the fee is probably worth it. This is much simpler and more cost effective if you do not need a large sum of money. Remember, your first withdrawals will have the highest amount of taxes attached to them.

Chapter 13

Annuities as an Insurance Product

Annuities are sold by insurance agencies for a reason: They are meant to insure you and your family's future. Dealing with insurance salesmen, however, can be an intimidating process. There is often stress associated with sales transactions, and there are many questions you will need to ask. Some insurance agents will even resort to high-pressure tactics in order to get you to part with your money. There is no need to be intimidated, though. The better educated you are, the more pointed questions you can ask and the more confident you will be during the sales process. Whatever sales situation you find yourself in, your knowledge regarding what you are up against will help you stay on top of your future.

Why are Insurance Agents Hounding Me About Investing?

Insurance agencies sell annuities because they are an insurance product. This does not make them any less valuable of an investment vehicle. Insurance agents may call you, or depending on the state, may even stop by your home to try to sell you annuities. They appear eager because agents earn a commission off your premium. When you buy an annuity through an insurance company, the person who sold it to you is entitled to a portion, around 5 percent, of your premium. This may discourage you, but remember, the bank officer or financial adviser who sells you an annuity also gets paid a percentage of your purchase. No matter where you go to purchase a financial product, be it an annuity, a CD, or even stocks and bonds, someone will make money off your purchase. This is just the nature of the financial world.

Insurance agents may not seem like the most appropriate individuals to give you financial advice, and unless they are **Series 6 certified**, they should not. The Series 6 license allows financial representatives to legally sell mutual funds and variable annuities. In order to be licensed in whichever state they are selling insurance, agents must pass a series of rigorous exams that test their knowledge, ranging from insurance products to annuities and the laws that govern the selling of these financial products. So, do not fret thinking that insurance agents are not knowledgeable about the products they sell. But, if you feel more comfortable going through a financial adviser, do it.

Insurance company ratings

This topic has briefly been touched upon already. Independent agencies rate insurance agencies so consumers will know the strength of the company they are investing in. The three most widely used companies are A.M. Best Co., Standard & Poor's, and Moody's. Each company ranks insurance companies in a slightly different manner. Factors like the insurance company's investments, claims history, and the volume of sales they conduct are all taken into account. Each rating agency has slightly different criteria for grading insurance companies. The following chart details what each agency looks for when doling out their ratings.

A.M. Best: A++ is the highest rating available. This signifies that the insurance company is superior to other companies. The C+ rating labels a company as marginal and should be avoided. The A.M. Best website can be found at **www.ambest.com.**

Standard & Poor's: AAA is the highest rank available through S&P. The rating of BB is reserved for marginal companies with inferior products and lower reliability. Their website is available at **www.standardandpoors.com.**

Moody's: A rating of Aaa is the highest rating available, meaning the company is exceptional. Rankings go down to Ba3, a label that says the company is of questionable worth. You can find more information on their website, **www.moodys.com.**

COMPANY	TOP RATING	WHAT THE RATINGS MEAN
A.M. Best	A++	Shows financial strength, either interactively or noninteractively.
Standard & Poor's	AAA	Grades financial strength along with insurance company's willingness to pay out on claims.
Moody's	Aaa	Shows financial strength and insurer's efficiency regarding claims.

In short, when looking for an insurance company, you will want to look for a company with A ratings. B and C companies may offer higher rates, but for some reason, they have been labeled as inferior companies, and it is recommended that you avoid them. It is probably in your best interest to go with the lower rate in exchange for a higher degree of stability. There are still plenty of competitive companies within the "A" range. If you do your homework, you will find them.

Avoiding Probate

When you pass away, your estate is taxable to your heirs as earnings. On top of this, your debts also become due. Any back taxes you may owe or any mortgages not settled will become your heirs' responsibility. There are ways to maximize the legacy you leave behind, though, and annuities can play a major role in this.

In most cases, annuities will pass on tax-free to your beneficiary in the event you pass away before the payout of your annuity is completed. This is one of the main features that make annuities an insurance product. Like life insurance, annuities will pass on to your beneficiary tax-free. However, depending on the annuitization options you choose, they may be limited in how they can access the money. They will also be responsible for any taxes you would be responsible for with your investment. This makes annuities a poor replacement for life insurance when it comes to passing on a gift to loved ones.

Death benefits

If you do wish to leave behind an estate, annuities certainly can be used for this purpose. Life insurance, however, is designed more specifically to fulfill this purpose. Go over your insurance options with your agent, and make sure you are getting the most value out of your investments. And, remember that annuities are designed primarily as retirement investments. If you wish to leave behind money for your heirs, consider purchasing separate life insurance. Not only is it cheaper, but you will be able to give your beneficiary a greater sum of money than you would be able to with an annuity.

With deferred annuities, the beneficiary will receive either the premium amount or the current cash value of the annuity, whichever one is greater. It should be made clear, however, that any loans, withdrawals, or fees will be subtracted from the death benefit amount.

There are some variable annuities out there that feature what is called an enhanced **death benefit**. This feature guarantees a death benefit that is higher than the actual contract amount. There is normally a small percentage that the principal amount will be increased by each year. Once the annuitant reaches a certain age, around 80 years old, the enhanced benefit disappears. This feature closely resembles universal life insurance, a fluctuating form of whole life insurance, and would be addressed in the prospectus. If your account performs poorly and you pass away unexpectedly, this benefit would be of great use.

Another variation of the standard death benefit is the stepped up death benefit. This rider forces the insurance company to pay out the highest cash value that the variable annuity reached during the life of the contract. For example, if the current cash value of the annuity at the time of the annuitant's death is $150,000, but two years prior the annuity was at $200,000, the higher amount would be paid to the beneficiary.

One final alternative is the return of premium death benefit. This is, again, only relevant for variable annuities. With this rider, the contract would state that no matter how much the market drops after the purchase of the annuity, the amount paid into it would be made payable to a beneficiary. Any withdrawals or fees would be subtracted from the original premium, but market losses would not affect the payout.

These benefits allow a certain degree of aggressiveness in **asset allocation**. Because your final expenses are guaranteed, you can afford to be a touch more eager with your investments. Again, these benefits are not free; you will most likely pay a fee for them so make sure to ask your insurance agent about this. In addition to this, some benefits may disappear once you annuitize your contract.

Beneficiaries

Naming a beneficiary for your annuity is covered when you fill out the contract paperwork. The beneficiary is not to be confused with the annuitant. The person who the annuity is originally set up for is the annuitant. The beneficiary is the one who receives the money if the annuitant dies. Depending on the contract, the beneficiary may either receive the annuity money in one lump sum or payments structured in the manner the annuitant received distributions.

If you have lost a loved one, your annuity is probably the farthest thing from your mind, but if your deceased spouse is still listed as a beneficiary, your annuity could be jeopardized in the event that you suddenly pass away. Make sure you review who is listed as your beneficiary periodically, especially if you have lost a loved one. The last thing you want is to have your family miss out on the money you have saved for them. One easy way to avoid extra paperwork is to simply name a contingent beneficiary when signing the original contract. This will also protect you if you and your primary beneficiary are killed in the same accident. The contingent will automatically receive any proceeds if your primary beneficiary cannot.

Stretch annuities

Stretch annuities are rare, as they are only offered by a few insurance companies. Also known as legacy annuities, this type of investment acts more like life insurance than an annuity because they are passed on to an heir. The main appeal of this annuity is that they pass on tax-free to a chosen beneficiary. The beneficiary can choose what to do with the money, whether it is keeping the annuity in the tax-deferred account or starting withdrawals.

Basically, stretch annuities are bought with either a single premium or flexible premiums and are never annuitized. When the original annuitant passes, their beneficiary will receive the annuity. The principal is received tax-free, and the beneficiary only pays taxes on the earnings. This is a simple way to pass money onto an heir without incurring a large tax burden.

Protection from creditors

If you have debt, an annuity will be protected from the reach of creditors. This is true even in the event that you pass away. Because annuities are insurance products, rather than becoming part of your estate when you pass away, the money passes to a beneficiary. This leaves them exempt from creditors, such as mortgage, credit card, or car loan lenders.

Utilizing the free look period

As discussed previously, all annuities offer a **free look period** during which the owner of the annuity has the right to back out of the contract. This time should be used to fix any mistakes that may have occurred. If you are happy with the contract, you have no need to act. If there is anything that arouses your suspicion, however, do not hesitate to contact the agency. If this does not help, it may be a good idea to withdraw your money and find a more beneficial contract. A typical free look period is 30 days.

Risk pools

A risk pool classifies a large group of people and attempts to find the longevity risk associated with the group. Obviously, not everyone lives to the national age expectancy. Some people live for shorter periods and some for longer. Risk pooling groups them all together and finds an average. If the number of cases is large enough, according to the **law of large numbers**, life expectancy can be estimated for the "average" individual. This is how life insurance and annuity rates are calculated. By no means does this method claim to predict the life of one person; rather, the focus is on the overall average. If the pool is large enough, everything will even out.

Life insurance is simple when it comes to adjusting to a risk pool calculation. Older folks will pay more for their insurance than a younger person would when applying for the same amount simply because the insurance company would not make any money if this were not the case.

Annuities are a bit trickier. The premium for an annuity is the amount invested, rather than a payment to the insurance company. Insurance companies battle the risk involved in selling annuities with a **mortality and expense risk fee**. This fee is the largest fee you will be charged, accounting for up to 1.75 percent of your initial investment. Calculated by mortality tables, which determine the odds of living to a certain age, this fee is there to protect the company if an individual lives longer than expected. If the investor does not live up to their expected age, the insurance company pockets the profits. With a 1.75 percent mortality and expense fee, a $100,000 investment would be charged $1,750 right at the beginning of the contract. This is most often a one-time charge, but it is a significant one. The remaining $98,250 would hopefully regain this amount within a year, but if the market sours, it may be several years before you are back to even.

Annuities offer something that savings cannot because of their risk pooling. This phenomenon is known as **survivorship credits**, which are comprised of three components: the original investment, any interest gained by that investment, and the money that was not used by those who died early in their contract period. Rather than going broke paying for those who live longer than expected, insurance companies use survivorship credits to help pay for those who live on late into their retirement. This "extra" money is partially funded by mortality and expense risk fees. Survivorship credits come from the money that is not used by those who pass away prior to receiving all the money that was owed to them.

One other factor in risk pooling is the sex of the investor. Statistically, women live longer than men. This means that in straight life annuities, they will receive less money than a man in the exact same risk category would. The mortality tables that insurance companies use give women about five years more of life than they do men. Because of this, women are given less money per month in distributions. In theory, this is because they will make up for the lost money during their extra years of life. This is not the case for every individual, but the statistics prove that this evens out when looking at a broad enough population.

Annuities as a Funding Source

Annuities are sometimes used in the insurance world as a method of funding other types of insurance. It is not uncommon for insurance professionals to set up an annuity in order to supply the premiums for life or long-term care insurance. The way it works is simple: A lump sum of money is used to purchase an annuity, whether it be fixed or variable. When the annuity matures and is ready to annuitize, rather than the owner of the annuity receiving distributions, the proceeds would instead go to the insurance company in order to pay the premiums for a different policy. Some individuals find this method to be an easier way of paying insurance bills because they will be covered for the rest of their lives by the annuity. It is also one less bill they will be personally responsible for.

Long-term care insurance is something that is rapidly gaining popularity. Because the cost of staying in a long-term care facility, such as a nursing home, is very expensive, long-term care insurance has found a strong foothold in the senior community. Depending on the level of care and freedom necessary, long-term care may cost as much as $75,000 per year. The rates for long-term care insurance are obviously much lower than this. The payouts from an annuity, depending on the size of the annuity, may be able to offset this monthly premium, which allows the investor one more degree of freedom in his or her daily life.

Sheltering income

An annuity is a legitimate way to shelter your income from taxes. If you are in a high tax bracket, you may want to consider an annuity to delay paying taxes on a large amount of money. Both fixed and variable annuities are appropriate for this, depending on your needs and characteristics. If you have just put the money in a CD, a fixed annuity would be more beneficial because you will delay paying taxes on the amount and will hopefully have a higher rate of return. Variable annuities are more beneficial for the active trader. This way you can have active control over your investment and avoid capital gains taxes, at least for the time being.

Medical underwriting

Because annuities are insurance products, they are subject to medical **underwriting**, a process used to assign a risk category to the applicant and then provide him or her with what the insurance company decides is an adequate amount of coverage. If the insurance company deems that the proposed insured is a health risk, he or she may qualify for lower premiums or higher distributions. Health insurance works quite similarly. When applying for a new health insurance policy, insurance companies may choose to not cover certain ailments because they manifested prior to the start of coverage. The poorer the health of the insured, the higher the rates will be.

This is the exact opposite of how life insurance works. If you are in poor health and apply for life insurance, you will have to pay more money for less coverage.

Life insurance and annuities

Whole life insurance policies can be surrendered after a specified length of time — usually two years — for a cash value. Because this often results in a loss when compared to the premiums paid, a variable annuity may be a better option. With a 1035 exchange, the investor can transfer his or her life insurance policy to an annuity. Although there would still be an immediate loss, it is more than likely the loss will be recovered after a few years. For example, assume Steve paid $5,000 in premiums for a whole life policy and the cash value after three years was at $3,000. If the interest rate is a steady 8 percent, it will take seven years to recoup the loss. Although this may not appeal to most, it does free up money if an emergency occurs.

It also can prevent a great loss in taxes. Steve's cost basis for the annuity would have been $5,000 for tax purposes. Once that money is recovered through the annuity, Steve would have virtually gained $2,000 of lost money, free from being taxed a second time.

You cannot convert an annuity to life insurance with a 1035 exchange. This does not mean it is impossible to do so, though; it only means the investor making the transfer will be responsible for any taxes and penalties incurred by cashing out the annuity. This option should not be taken lightly. A large number of elderly citizens do not qualify for affordable life insurance because they are viewed upon as a high-risk demographic. Although it is true that most life insurance policies will have a superior pay-in to pay-out ratio for beneficiaries than annuities do, it is not an option for everyone. The older you are, the more expensive your life insurance is going to be. There are also medical conditions, such as insulin dependent diabetes, that automatically disqualify people from life insurance approval.

CASE STUDY: MANAGING YOUR RISK AND PRESERVING WEALTH

Robert Riedl
Director of Wealth Management,
Sumnicht & Associates
www.sumnicht.com

For Robert Riedl, annuities are more than just a way to save money for retirement. Sumnicht & Associates, LLC is a family wealth management firm that specializes in managing risk and preserving family wealth for future generations. They recommend the purchase of a combination of life insurance and annuities to their elderly high-net worth clients. As the director of wealth management, Riedl assists clients to preserve their estate for heirs while minimizing estate taxes. By employing annuities with life insurance products, the client receives a steady monthly income from the annuity, and the taxable portion of an estate is drastically reduced by the life insurance. This allows retirees to alleviate their worries about market risk on their portfolio while maximizing the transfer of their accumulated wealth to their heirs. Sumnicht & Associates is not affiliated directly with any insurance company; rather, they will shop around in order to provide the best possible financial return for their clients.

The process that Riedl uses involves the use of life insurance, combined with the purchase of an annuity. First of all, in order for this insurance arbitrage to work, the client must be in good health to qualify for life insurance. With a growing number of retirees being more and more healthy, insurability is fast becoming a non-issue. Once they have proven they are in fact insurable, Riedl requires that they be a few years into their retirement, preferably around age 75 to 85 years old so they can achieve a higher monthly income from the annuity. Basically, the higher the age, the higher the monthly income, the greater the annual return on the annuity. Because annuities are technically an insurance policy, the life insurance proceeds will go directly to his or her heirs after the annuitant passes away without being locked up in probate or estate taxes.

The goal is to find the highest degree of arbitrage available. This process involves buying a large single-premium immediate annuity, as well as a significant amount of life insurance. In the example Riedl gives, the hypothetical $2.5 million annuity would pay out $24,175 per month for the rest of "Jack's" life. In order to preserve the same $2.5 million for his heirs, however, a $2.5-million whole life insurance policy would also need to be purchased. This policy would cost $10,189 per month, leaving Jack $13,986 per month — a 9 percent rate of return before taxes. If $2,723 of the money went to taxes, this would leave a 5.4 percent return, a rate the vast majority of other investment products cannot come near to matching.

While this is only an example, it illustrates how these insurance products are related in offering the maximum benefits not only to an annuitant but also to the annuitant's beneficiaries.

The purchase of an annuity is not something to be taken lightly. It is a major decision affecting your finances, possibly for the rest of your life. By becoming more familiar with the purchasing process and the players involved, you will be better suited to make a decision. You can begin your search by contacting a local insurance agent or simply by logging on to the Internet. There are literally thousands of annuities out there; you just need to find the one that best matches your needs. The more informed you are about every aspect of the annuity you are thinking of purchasing — from its features to its penalties — the easier the process will be.

Chapter 14

Purchasing an Annuity

Betty answered the phone only to be greeted by a friendly insurance agent. The agent claimed he had sent Betty a piece of literature concerning annuities in the mail, and although Betty did not remember receiving the parcel, she was curious enough to agree to meet the agent in person. When the agent finished his description of the product, he showed Betty an illustration of how her $100,000 could support her for the rest of her life with an annuity. Then, the agent just sat there expectantly looking at her.

If the previous situation would make you uncomfortable, you are not alone. The approach used by the agent dealing with Betty in the previous example is known in sales circles as the silent close and has proved to be very effective. It works because it puts the prospect in an uncomfortable position. He or she is willing to do anything to break the silence, even if it means purchasing something he or she does not truly want.

Annuities are purchased from either an insurance company or from a financial services firm. It is important to be familiar with the annuities sales force and the steps involved in purchasing these products before you actually purchase them. The above example is an extreme case, but it does happen from time to time.

By knowing what you are up against, you will be more prepared to make the right decisions. Remember, your agent should be putting your best interests first. If he of she is not, find a new agent.

Who will I Buy an Annuity From?

In most cases, the annuity purchaser will have direct contact with an individual sales representative or a captive agent who represents a larger firm or company. In order to sell fixed annuities, the agent must be licensed to sell life insurance in that particular state. For variable annuities, the agent must also have a securities license. This separate license is necessary because variable annuities involve a degree of risk. Remember, variable annuities can fluctuate up or down depending on market conditions.

Agents may contact you via phone or through mailings. With the advent of the national do-not-call registry, cold calling is quickly becoming outdated. Most representatives now work through referrals, meaning agents may have provided their services to an acquaintance of yours who gave them your name. Do not be surprised when the agent you meet with asks you for the names of others who could benefit from these products.

It must be realized that most insurance agents work solely off **commission**. This means they will not charge you for their sales meeting. It also means they are paid when the client purchases something from them. Do not be intimidated with the high-pressure sales tactics that some agents may employ. Take your time, and absorb the information for the products they pitch. Compare that information with other products out there before you make a decision.

You do not need to make a decision right away, regardless of what sales tactics are used. Take your time, and make the decision that will benefit you the most.

Where Can I Buy an Annuity?

Nonqualified: If you are buying a nonqualified account, or in other words, an annuity with money that has already been taxed, nine times out of ten, you will be purchasing an annuity from an insurance company or an insurance agent. The companies you should be doing background research on will differ greatly, and it pays — literally — to know what you are up against. Sites like **www.annuityadvantage.com** will list the different products available from different companies in your state. This site also compares and contrasts annuity rates and the insurance company's overall strength rating.

Qualified: If you are purchasing an annuity through work, you will be buying a qualified account. This means the money you are using to buy the annuity has not yet been taxed. Even though you will be purchasing this type of annuity in the workplace, there are still a few different sales representatives you need to be familiar with.

Employer-sponsored plan managers are probably the most prevalent sales agents in this category. These agents may meet with you either privately or at work to go over your options. Normally, these accounts are maintained in conjunction with a 401(k) in order to give the annuitant better options when it comes time to tap into his or her accumulated assets. As the amount of companies offering pension plans declines, these sales reps are becoming more widespread. Plan managers may or may not earn a commission off your annuity purchase.

As far as dealing with insurance agents, you may want to consider an independent agent. An independent agent will have access to many different products and is not tied down to one particular company as captive agents are. Although independent agents may still be affiliated with particular companies, they technically are able to sell almost any product.

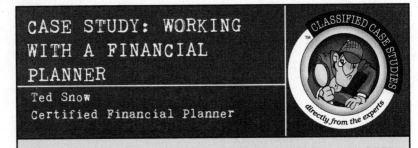

CASE STUDY: WORKING WITH A FINANCIAL PLANNER

Ted Snow
Certified Financial Planner

Ted Snow is an independent Certified Financial Planner (CFP) practitioner. Serving clients all over the country and in the Dallas area for almost 23 years as an insurance agent, Snow has the ability to sell products from many different insurance companies. This allows him to pick and choose the products that would best fit the needs of his clients. "Being independent, [and] offering no proprietary products, helps me to be objective so that my clients get the best value and benefit for their investment dollar," Snow said.

When he first contacts prospective clients, it is usually not to their surprise. Snow does not cold call people who have never heard of him; rather, he works mainly by preferred introductions. Prospective clients will approach him, or he will contact people whose names were provided to him by existing clients or centers of influence like CPAs. Either way, his prospective clients automatically have a higher degree of trust in Snow because he comes as a recommended adviser.

When it is actually time to present the different investment rec-ommendations to his clients, Snow does so on a "value-added" basis. Sometimes, several different products will be presented to the prospect. How does he know which product will be the best fit for an individual client? "It all depends on what features a client needs," Snow said. "Some annuities have a strong death benefit. Some have strong living benefits. Some have strong in-come benefits. Other annuities have better subaccounts to in-vest in than others." By representing more than one company, Snow has the ability to find an annuity that will fit a client's needs.

This involves a degree of knowledge that captive agents do not necessarily have. While captive agents represent just one company, Snow and other independent CFPs need to have a wider base of knowledge about the products available to them. In order to attain this, Snow meets periodically with representa-tives from particular companies to go over the products he may want to offer his clients. Combined with his own due diligence and with the help of his team, Snow learns the intricacies of the different products available to him. Any questions are resolved with further conversations with the respective annuity whole-sales, other financial planners in his office, and his current bro-ker/dealer.

Snow recommends a product only if he knows in his profes-sional opinion and experience it will be highly beneficial to the client. By recommending one or two annuities that would be a good fit, he narrows their search for the proper investment. Ul-timately, it is left up to the client to make the final decision. The more information he can give the client the better. By imparting this knowledge to a client, he or she is better able to make an investment decision.

The process does not end there. Snow meets with his clients at least twice a year to review their investments and annuity contracts. At this point, the performance of the product is as-sessed and the specific annuity living and death benefits are re-examined. This helps ensure the investment products continue to meet individual needs of the client. With so many products to choose from, sometimes a reallocation is necessary. If the market has since soured, perhaps a change to a more stable subaccount is needed.

The financial planning process does not need to be a scary thing. By working with a Certified Financial Planner practitioner or insurance professional who you trust, you will feel much more comfortable with your investment decisions. This security will help make your retirement years that much more stress-free.

Buying online

Thanks to the Internet, it is much easier to research and buy annuities, or any other financial or insurance product for that matter. Virtually every company out there has a website you can visit for more information. There are also independent watchdog sites that compare different companies and products, with **www.annuityadvantage.com** and **www.annuityfyi.com** being two of the more popular. Perusing these sites will not only help you find the annuity that best suits your needs, but it will also save you the time of meeting with several different agents.

With free annuity calculators, you can extrapolate how much return you would receive, both before and after taxes. On the best of these calculators, there are different variables you can add in, such as current age, annuitization age, initial premium, monthly contributions, and assumed interest rate. Knowing how much money you will need for retirement, as determined in the goals section earlier in this book, will let you know just what you need to do to reach your financial goals. One great annuity calculator can be found on Yahoo!®: **http://finance.yahoo. com/calculator/insurance/ins08.**

With the help of this online calculator, you can determine how much a tax-deferred account would earn over time and how much the same account would earn if there were no tax-deferral benefits. For example, a $10,000 initial investment, followed by $500 each year for 20 years, would be worth $49,608 at the end of the period assuming a consistent 8 percent interest rate and a tax rate of 28 percent. The same investment, under the same conditions, would be worth $71,321 in a tax-deferred account.

The most important thing to remember about annuity and other financial calculators is that they are based on the assumption that the past is predictive of the future. It is impossible to predict the future with 100 percent accuracy, even with fixed annuities, considering that market conditions dictate even the most stable of investments. If you are looking for the customer service provided by an actual agent, it is probably not in your best interest to purchase online annuities. This does not mean you should avoid doing your own research, though. The Internet is a valuable resource, regardless of how you choose to purchase an annuity.

When Should I Buy an Annuity?

If you do not need the money in the short term, anytime is a good time to purchase an annuity. There are, however, a few stages in life that benefit most from the security an annuity or annuities will provide, each age group benefiting in their own unique way.

Your 20s: At this age, retirement seems worlds away. But, this may be the best time to start. Although it is true that this age group has the most amount of debt, they also have the most potential for growth. A single premium of $10,000 invested at age 20 with a 6 percent rate of return and then accessed at age 65 is worth $135,698. Compare this scenario to a 30 year old making the same investment. The 30 year old accessing his or her investment with the same 6 percent rate of return at age 65 would only have $76,861, a touch more than half the amount that the 20 year old earned.

Your 30s: If you have not started planning for your retirement at this point, it is a good time to start. You will want to get an early start so you can have as comfortable a retirement as possible. A variable annuity would be great at this stage in your life because you can allocate your money in a fairly aggressive blend of subaccounts without worrying about the risk because you have so much earning potential left. Compounding interest will begin, and your annuity will start growing slowly.

Your 40s: The kids are growing up and going to college. Maybe there is a wedding coming up. You have expenses, but they are manageable thanks to your foresight. Your earning potential should be near its peak at this age. Tax deferral should sound awfully nice as you store away what money you can for your retirement. Besides, annuities are exempt from being claimed on your child's FAFSA form for college.

Your 50s: By this point, your nest egg should be a decent size. Your 401(k) and IRA should be at a very healthy size as well, and you might have extra money you wish to invest. An annuity with a guarantee, such as a fixed annuity or a guaranteed living benefit variable annuity, would be appropriate at this stage. Retirement is not too far away now; you need to protect the capital you worked so hard throughout your career to make. Your family's well being should be your No. 1 concern. Guarantees, such as the ones given with fixed annuities, will help you most of all. This does not mean all of your money should be in a fixed annuity, but enough of it should be there to protect your future. It is almost time to start living your dream.

Your 60s and 70s: You are retired, and the kids have moved out. You are active and have a good life ahead of you, but it is never too early to start thinking about your needs. An advance life deferred annuity sounds attractive because it will earn interest and pay well once you reach your 80s. If for some reason you do end up in a nursing home, and current statistics say that 50 percent of people will need some sort of long-term care at some point in their lives, the ALDA will take away some of the burden from your loved ones.

What do I Need to Buy an Annuity?

Purchasing an annuity is a different process than buying other insurance products. With life, health, or long-term care insurance, extensive medical tests are required to decide whether you fit into their insurability profile. With an annuity, you will only need:

- Some proof of your age and the money you wish to invest. Some companies require ongoing proof of survival for many years after the contract is signed. This is done to prevent the abuse of lifetime benefits and is administered by simply signing and dating an official form.

- A suitability form that adheres to industry financial health standards. This will prove the agent selling you your annuity did not recommend that you put an inappropriate percentage of your money into his or her product. This is merely a way for you to visualize more fully the investment and commitment you are making.

- Money. You cannot sign a contract without investing money into the annuity. For many companies, it is possible to do this with a direct debit from your checking or savings account so have your banking information at the ready.

As you can see, the process is not nearly as intense as the applications for these other types of insurance. There are no home nurse visits or examinations of your medical records necessary.

The Application Process

Like any insurance product, the annuity investor must fill out an application. These are straightforward, and the agent you meet with will likely fill most of it out for you. This is perfectly fine, as long as your signature appears on the application. If the annuitant and the owner are different people, both signatures are required. A third-party signature may be required if the owner is older than a certain age, normally 85.

The application questions are simple. The owner's and the annuitant's name, age, and contact information will all be included. The amount you are investing will also be stated here if it is a single premium contract. If you are transferring funds from a checking or savings account, the application may ask for a routing and account number so it can be directly debited from your account. By no means is this an obligation, but it does speed up the process. Finally, the agent will sign the application.

Things get a bit more complicated after the general application is completed. If there is going to be a 1035 exchange taking place, the agent needs to record the investor's authority to transfer funds. This part of the application will delve into more detail about your previous investment. The type of account, the most current balance (if known), and another signature are all required. The points of comparison between the old and the new contract must also be listed. This is for your protection; your new annuity should be more beneficial to you than the old one. Some states, such as New York, have more stringent rules regarding exchanges. Your agent will likely take care of the bulk of the paperwork if you are doing a 1035 exchange.

Another part of the application is the taxpayer identification. Your Social Security number or taxpayer identification number will be recorded, along with a statement that you do not owe any back taxes. This is required and is used as proof by the insurance company that you are not evading taxes.

The last piece of the application process is the annuity suitability form. This is a questionnaire regarding your finances and assets. Again, without this information, the agent cannot make a recommendation that will meet your needs. Agents must make an honest attempt to get your financial information, including any investment experience. You may not feel comfortable divulging this information, but it truly is necessary if you want the product that will best fit your needs. This is especially true in the case of a rollover or transfer from one annuity to another. The suitability form in this instance would include a list of the positive and negative aspects of transferring your money.

The contract

Annuities are more accurately defined as a contract than they are as an investment. Once your application is approved, your agent will deliver the contract to you. This is when the free look period begins. In most cases, this is proven by the insurance company with a receipt of delivery, which has both the signatures of you and your agent. The contract will look familiar to you; it should consist of the terms you and your agent went over during the sales meeting, as well as a facsimile of the application that was filled out. These are important papers — do not lose them. The contract will also have information on how to contact your insurance provider if you have any questions or concerns.

Investing as a routine

If you are serious about earning high rates of return, your best option is to invest more money. By periodically investing more money, you will create more wealth for yourself and your family. The easiest way to do so is by setting up a direct debit from your bank account to your flexible annuity. Dollar cost averaging will occur if you invest over a long enough period, and the fluctuations in the market prices will even out, letting you profit from the market's historically steady increases.

Some experts argue that when investing in variable accounts, you should always have cash on hand. This allows for a few different things to happen. One, you are better prepared in the event of an emergency. Having easily accessible funds will help you to avoid surrender fees and other penalties.

The second reason for keeping cash on hand is so you can invest larger amounts when the market is down. Although dollar cost averaging will account for inflation-related gains within variable annuities, investing more when the market is down has the potential to lead to even larger profits. This is not necessarily an easy thing to do

Other ideas for higher returns

There is more to investing than just putting money in your account. Some simple methods for investing are included below:

Watch for High Fixed Rates: There are fixed annuities out there that offer consistent high rates of return. Taking advantage of a 6- or 7-percent guaranteed rate will increase your capital, or liquid assets, much more quickly than the traditional 3 or 4 percent that fixed annuities offer.

Beware of Excessive Fees: This type of fee is like the treadmill you bought and never used — it was frivolous spending and took a chunk out of your income. There is no point in paying for annuity features you do not want or need. Cutting costs is a surefire way to increase your profits.

Reallocate when necessary: By keeping your assets where they benefit you the most, you maximize your earnings. This means adjusting where your money is kept on at least a yearly basis. A periodic review of your holdings may reveal that your subaccounts have shifted. Reallocating is simple and involves only minor labor on your part. If the market sours, it is very easy to shift aggressive accounts to cash accounts. Your agent will also be able to help you if you are unsure of what to do.

Chapter 15

Questions to Ask Your Agent

Your agent acts as the face of the insurance company. Pretty much any contact you have with the insurance company will be done through an agent. There are even agents out there who still deliver death benefits to grieving families. Whatever the agent's role is within his or her company, he or she should be able to fully explain the products he or she sells. Most of the time though, you will need to ask the right questions to get the information necessary in making a decision.

Still, going out and meeting the annuity sales force can be a daunting task. A few pushy salesmen, high costs, and inferior products have given the entire insurance industry a bad reputation. Although there are some unethical insurance agents, most insurance agents who you come across are not of this ilk and would never dream of taking advantage of you. Either way, you can rest assured that you will be prepared. This chapter includes a few quick points of comparison that will help make your decision making process a touch easier.

What will this Annuity do for Me?

This might be the most important question to ask. Your insurance agent should be well versed in the advantages of the annuity you are considering. He or she should also know the negative aspects involved. If possible, ask for a side-by-side comparison of the pros and cons of the annuity you are considering. If you are not happy with the negatives, do not buy the annuity. There is truly an annuity out there for everyone — why should you settle for something that will not meet your needs?

What Kind of Annuity am I Interested in?

This is a broad question that actually encompasses three smaller questions:

- How and when am I paying for this annuity?

- When will I start receiving distributions?

- Where is the money that I am purchasing this annuity with coming from?

These questions will breakdown the annuity into the three main categories; they may seem familiar. The above questions can also be phrased as having:

- Single or flexible premiums?

- Immediate or deferred earnings?

- Qualified or nonqualified contributions?

What Rate is the Company Paying on Older Annuities?

This question may seem obscure, but it can give you an idea of the company's financial consistency. If they are paying existing annuities at a much lower rate than they are offering you, it may be a signal that your annuity's rate may not stay high for long. A company may offer a minimum rate of 3 percent with a bonus rate of an additional 3.5 percent to give new annuitants a 6.5 percent rate total for the first year of their annuity. Although this seems fine, the annuitants may be shocked once the second year of their annuity kicks in and the rate is lowered to 4 percent.

What is the Guaranteed Interest Rate?

This question is important because it clearly establishes a minimum rate of return. If the company suffers, it may very well be paying you this rate. Be sure to ask for illustrations demonstrating the minimum interest rate alongside the current one. This will allow you to see the range of what you will earn — both the best case and worst case scenarios. If a company guarantees a rate of 4 percent but offers twice that as the current rate, you will want an illustration that shows both ends of the spectrum. Because it is unlikely the company can maintain an 8 percent rate for long, you will want to know what the bare minimum amount is that will be returned to you.

With a $10,000 single premium, you can expect a return of $78,311 after 35 years with an 8 percent initial rate and an average rate of 6 percent afterward. However, with an investment that only performs at 4 percent after the first year, your return will almost be half as much: $40,979. You very well could be given only the minimum so it definitely pays to know what your annuity's distribution range will be.

How Strong is the Company?

Your insurance agent should know how fiscally strong the company he or she works for is. Each year, companies are subject to solvency requirements, as set forth by each state's insurance superintendent. On top of this, you should also do your own research. Outside companies, such as A.M. Best, rate insurance companies as to their overall strength. At the very least, your agent should know their company's rating.

How Long is the Free Look Period?

Laws vary from state to state regarding how many days you have to return the policy and receive the entire amount invested back without penalties or fees. This is also known as the right to return period. This is the time for you to read your final contract very carefully. If there is anything you do not agree with, or if there are any errors, the free look period provides you time to return the contract and get your money back. The free look period should be displayed prominently in your contract.

What are the Surrender Charges on Nonscheduled Withdrawals?

Remember, it is vital for you to understand that annuities are long-term investments, but emergencies do arise. Unexpected medical bills, family emergencies, or just a rash of bad luck may require you to make a withdrawal from your annuity before you are scheduled to. You might not intend to make an early withdrawal when purchasing the annuity, but it may very well happen. It is important to know ahead of time what kind of penalty you will pay.

Many states have laws that enable you to make nonscheduled withdrawals of up to 10 percent without facing a penalty, with New York being one of the most prominent. Another way around surrender charges is to simply annuitize your investment a bit earlier than originally intended. As long as you are past the minimum age of 59½, you will not be penalized. Still, you should know what the surrender period schedule looks like in the event that you must access your money early. You will also want to ask if there are exceptions to the surrender period in the event of terminal illness or convalescent care.

Are there Additional Fees?

Surrender charges may be just the beginning of the fees that an insurance company is looking to collect. With fixed annuities, the fees are built into the interest rate awarded, but it is a much different story with variable annuities. There are commission charges, usually taken out as a fraction of your account balance. Although these fees are not hefty — 1 or 2 percent — they do add up quickly. If you are uncomfortable with these fees, you may want to do some further searching for annuities with a lower rate.

In addition to commission fees, there will sometimes be a service charge or an administrative fee. This can be expressed either as a percentage of the balance, or more commonly, a straight dollar amount.

When Will Distributions Begin?

This is largely determined by you, the owner of the annuity. Most companies will not have you choose when you want to receive distributions with fixed or variable annuities until you are ready to annuitize your investment. Once you reach age 59½, you can elect to annuitize your contract at any time. At this time, you will need to decide whether you want monthly or yearly distributions. You will also need to choose the type of distribution you wish to receive. The difference between a straight life distribution and a joint and survivor distribution becomes very important at this stage in the annuity process.

How Do I Change My Policy?

In most cases, this will be stipulated in the contract. If it is a simple change, such as a different beneficiary, usually a quick note to your insurance agent can cover this. If it is a major change, such as a change in the structuring of your annuity, you will need to have written authorization from the president of the company. To save you time and stress, it is a much better idea to shop around and find the contract that best fits your needs. This is due to the fact that changing your annuity is quite difficult after the fact. It is almost always better to spend a bit of extra time and find the annuity that best suits you.

What Riders are Available to Me?

Some riders may be included for free along with the annuity contract, while the company may charge you for others. Riders allow you to customize your annuity so it fully meets your needs. If you are charged for something you do not particularly want or need, you may have purchased the wrong annuity. It is important you know ahead of time what you are getting for your money, and thus, what riders are included in the cost of your annuity. When dealing with variable annuities, living benefits are usually considered riders, and although they may be beneficial, they come at a cost. It is important to make sure you find value in the benefits offered.

What Do I Do if I Have a Complaint or Question that my Company Does not Address?

Insurance companies are regulated by their particular state's insurance department. If you have a question or complaint that your company does not answer or address, contact the state officials. Each state's insurance regulator has a website, and a simple Web search will help you find the proper regulator.

Chapter 16

Structuring Your Annuity

You will want to receive payments from an annuity in a way that best suits your needs. After all, you put the money into the annuity in order to receive profits from it down the road. By structuring the distributions of your annuity to match your lifestyle, you will set yourself up for success in your retirement. You will also want to make sure the groundwork is established so that if something were to happen to you, your heirs will receive the money you intended for them to have.

Retirement Planning

Individuals are able to receive social security benefits starting at age 62. As retirees age, the amount they would receive becomes greater, capping at age 66. Social Security, however, only provides a percentage of what the individual's income was during his or her working years. This may not be enough for the retiree to enjoy the lifestyle he or she wishes to have post-retirement. For most, some other source of income is necessary. Both IRAs and 401(k)s can provide for such needs, but these financial vehicles do not provide a guaranteed income for life like annuities do.

Because of this, even the most prepared investor should consider owning an annuity.

Payouts

Most insurance companies do not ask you to set up a payout structure when you first sign the annuity contract with deferred annuities. This is done once you decide to annuitize the investment. If it is an immediate annuity, you are choosing to annuitize the investment within a year of purchasing it. For these contracts, your insurance agent should help you decide how and when to receive distributions upon signing.

The most important things to think about when you are deciding how to structure the distributions from your annuity are the goals you set forth prior to purchasing it. Is the annuity a necessity for the expenses of daily living? If so, you will want sufficient monthly or quarterly distributions in order to meet that need. Is the annuity intended to be a gift for a loved one? In this case, you may want to only withdraw the interest gained and leave the principal amount alone so your loved ones will receive a tax-free sum of money upon your death.

Many people wonder how much of their assets they should put into an annuity. This largely depends on how much you have, what your expenses are, and if you have other sources of income. You do not want to tie up money you will need soon. You also do not want to lock emergency funds up if it will cost you to get the money out. In short, no one can determine what is best for you but you. A good insurance agent will help you determine your goals and walk you through each step of this process.

When dealing with variable annuities, one attractive option available is the level payment. This type of distribution from your contract would lock in a specific amount you would receive for a given length of time, normally a year. At the end of each year, the payout would change in order to keep up with how the subaccounts you chose were responding to any market changes. This type of distribution works best for investors who worry about short-term fluctuations within the market. Rather than reflecting how the chosen section of the market performed each month, results are tallied up at the end of each 12-month period.

For example, assume you own a variable annuity that is connected to the S&P 500. If the index begins the year at 1,000 points, dips down to 800 during August, yet finishes the year back at 1,000, the amount received per distribution would drop slightly to reflect the short drop in the index. It is impossible to completely shield yourself from a short-term drop in the market. But, the large drop in funds distributed back to you during the one bad month would be substituted by a more steady and uniform distribution.

Distribution Options

Your distribution options are the features that inform you of the choices that the insurance company gives regarding the repayment of your investment. Most insurance companies will not have you choose how you want to be repaid until you are ready to begin the payout portion of your contract, but you should still be aware of the choices you have because this is not the case with all companies. The more aware you become of the end result of your annuity, the better of a planning job you can have regarding your retirement prior to needing the money. This will ensure a more worry-free retirement. You have various annuitization choices as an investor, which will allow you to customize your distributions so they may best suit your retirement needs.

Straight life

This is the oldest and most basic form of an annuity. All distributions go to the annuitant only and are made for the entire duration of the annuitant's life. Once the annuitant dies, distributions will completely cease. Because there is no death benefit for heirs, this policy offers the highest rate of return to the annuitant while he or she is living. If you want to leave something behind for a beneficiary however, this is probably not the best option for you.

Life with period certain

This option will pay the annuitant for the rest of his or her life as well. The annuitant, however, is able to select a period over which the remaining portion of the annuity will be distributed to a beneficiary in the event of his or her premature death. The period starts at the beginning of the annuity contract, and if the annuitant dies within that period, the remainder of the annuity will then be distributed to the annuitant's beneficiary. This option ranges between five and 25 years. Distributions to heirs can be done as either one lump-sum payment or in the same fashion the annuitant received distributions. This is determined by the contract the annuitant agreed to at the annuities initiation.

Because there is a death benefit, this type of annuity distribution will pay slightly less per distribution than a straight life option. As with any benefit to an annuity, there are trade-offs made in returns.

Period certain

Under this payment option, the annuity's distributions will take place under a set period. Most companies limit this period from between five to 25 years. Annuity distributions will continue for the predetermined period regardless of whether the annuitant is living. In this case, additional payments, if the specified period has not yet elapsed, will go to the annuitant's beneficiary.

Amount certain

Annuitants are able to choose how much they would like to receive per distribution with this option. This is determined by the amount they put into the annuity and how long they wish to receive their distributions. In the event of the annuitant's death, if there is still money left in the annuity, the remainder goes to the beneficiary. Because you are actually able to choose how much you wish to receive, this type of contract does not extend for the life of an annuitant. Instead, the distributions continue at the specified amount until there is nothing left within the annuity. The death benefit would only be collected by a beneficiary if there is money left in the annuity account upon the passing away of the annuitant.

Joint and survivor

With this option, two lives are covered by a single annuity contract. This payout plan is mainly used by married couples. The most popular option gives 100 percent of the regular distributions to the surviving spouse for the remainder of his or her life. Available to both fixed and variable annuity owners, this can be extremely beneficial to the survivor when dealing with final expenses of the deceased spouse and the continued cost of living.

Flexible annuitization

An innovative and new approach to payouts called flexible annuitization gives investors much more control over how they receive their money. With this distribution option, annuitants can elect to have a set amount of their investment that will be returned to them for a selected number of years. The rest of the investment is accessible at any time regardless of surrender periods. This allows the investor to withdraw money as needed in case of an emergency, while still providing him or her with regular distributions and a competitive rate of return on the investment. The entire amount of the investment gains interest at the specified contract rate, as opposed to just the amount to be annuitized. This feature has helped annuities become more competitive with other investment products that allow easy access to money, such as money market accounts and mutual funds.

Guaranteed living benefits

A living benefit rider is an add-on used in variable annuities. There are several different variations of these living benefits. Remember, these are extras and because of this, they will most often come at a cost to the owner. Still, they may prove to be exactly what you need. If this is the case, you should strongly consider opting for one of them, assuming the corresponding fee is acceptable in light of your financial needs.

Guaranteed Minimum Income Benefit: This option gives you the opportunity to choose between a guaranteed minimum rate of return or the market value of your investment, whichever is most beneficial. This type of annuity rider is uncommon because it combines the main feature of a fixed annuity with all of the benefits of a variable annuity. There is a ten-year minimum deferment with this rider, meaning you cannot access your money without a hefty penalty for the first ten years of the contract. If you need an immediate source of income, this is not the right choice for you.

Guaranteed Minimum Withdrawal Benefit: This provides investors with a guaranteed distribution amount that they will receive each month for the duration of the payout phase. If the market performs better than expected, toward the end of the distribution period, all excess funds will be distributed back to the annuitant. However, if the market performs poorly, your initial premium will not be lost. The insurance company takes the brunt of the risk with this type of rider. A typical withdrawal ranges from 6 to 12 percent of your original investment. The industry average is roughly 14 years of distributions, assuming your annuity does not lose value over the course of your investment.

Guaranteed Lifetime Withdrawal Benefit: For as long as the annuitant is alive, he or she can withdraw a certain percentage of his or her investment. Oftentimes, there will be a minimum amount guaranteed with this type of living benefit rider. This guarantee is for the entire lifetime of the annuitant. This rider takes all of the positive aspects of a guaranteed minimum income benefit and a guaranteed minimum withdrawal benefit, and then adds to it a lifetime guarantee that your money will not run out.

Guaranteed Payout Annuity Floor: This rider guarantees that distribution amounts will never fall less than a certain percentage of the first distribution. This rider is fairly new and applies to variable annuities only. Its main purpose is to protect the investor from poor markets during the payout phase so that even if the market tanks, the investor will still receive a large distribution from his or her annuity.

Guaranteed Account Value: With this rider, your account is guaranteed to not fall less than a certain amount, regardless of how poorly the market performs. Any gains are locked in for the period selected. Normally, this benefit is only available for the first few years of the contract in order to weather any short-term market losses. A typical guaranteed account value would be for ten years. Again, this rider is only for variable annuities and is used mainly as the variable annuity response to an equity-indexed annuity because it locks in market gains and does not change even if the market sours. A typical surrender period for this type of annuity ranges from five to ten years.

Guaranteed Minimum Accumulation Benefit: This option guarantees your principal investment. If, at the end of a certain period — around ten years — your account has lost value, you will receive your principal investment back. If there are gains on your account, you would receive those — plus principal — instead. This option does have what are known as "step-ups." With a step-up, the investor has a greater amount guaranteed to be returned to him or her. For example, suppose the market has consistently performed well for a $250,000 initial investment so that after ten years, it is now $400,000. The annuity contract may include a clause that after ten years, whatever the gains have been in the annuity are now guaranteed alongside the initial investment. Therefore, with this step-up, the account is now guaranteed for $400,000, no matter how poorly the market performs afterward.

For-Life Benefits: This option allows annuitants to receive a percentage of their original investment back for as long as they live. The newest living benefit available to investors, this benefit even allows for investment growth if the account value were to increase. A typical account would have these increases credited every three to five years. Because this option is age-based, younger investors will pay a higher fee than older investors.

If an investor had $500,000 as his or her original investment, he or she would be eligible to receive roughly $25,000, or 5 percent, each year for life. If the investment increased in value over time, the yearly — or monthly — distributions would increase accordingly. This benefit is only applicable after you choose to annuitize your contract.

Premium Bonuses: In addition to the above living benefits, there is another more generic option that an insurance company might offer. Premium bonuses have become a very popular benefit. These premium bonuses will instantly add money to your account, just for signing the contract. In the past, there have been some that offer as much as 10 percent of the amount deposited into your annuity on top of your premium. Premium bonuses have either higher fees or longer surrender periods. Nonetheless, they may be worth it based on the time frame in which you will need the funds. If you are investing for a long period, the surrender period will have been surpassed, and your investment will return to you penalty-free.

Rate Bonuses: Some annuities, rather than just giving you a percentage of your premium as a bonus, add on an additional few points to the interest rate of return. For example, if the annuity normally earns 3 percent, the insurance company might add on an additional 3 percent for the duration of the first year.

Living benefits address the main problem with variable annuities: the fact that your investment can completely disappear if your asset allocation is wrong. Because of this, living benefits have a strong appeal to those who are not happy with the minimal returns of fixed annuities.

But, living benefits come at a cost besides the extra fees. Your choice of the subaccounts available to you may be severely limited because the insurance companies do not want you to risk money they are guaranteeing by putting your money into a riskier subaccount. Your risk taking may result in a loss for the insurance company because of the benefits they would be obliged to pay even though your money had dissipated. This forces insurance companies to place restrictions on your choice of subaccounts. These restrictions should be taken into account, but that does not necessarily mean you should avoid annuities with premium bonuses. If you are a fairly conservative investor, there will be little change to your options, seeing as how the riskier investments would have been avoided anyway.

How rates are determined

Financial companies use complicated formulas to determine the rates and fees of their annuity products. Different types of annuities will have different charges. The company's fiscal health also plays a big role in the determination of these charges. Questions, such as how well the company's investments performed and how much revenue was created through other sales, also play a big role.

You must remember, though, that the agent selling a policy is going to be compensated one way or another. With variable annuities, this is a transparent process. These policies will have a maintenance charge built right in, either as a percentage of premium or a fixed dollar amount. With fixed annuities, though, the fee is not so easily determined. The rate of return the investor will see is artificially lowered to compensate the company and the agent responsible for the sale.

Monthly versus Annually

How often do you wish to receive your distributions? If you are receiving monthly social security benefits already, you may not need to receive distributions from your annuity on a monthly basis as well and should instead let the funds sit and gain interest for a longer period. Or, you may find that your social security is not quite enough and may need supplemental money halfway through the month. Again, this is something you will have to sit down and decide for yourself.

If you are using the annuity to fund another type of insurance, you may want to receive distributions on a yearly basis because an annual premium will reduce the amount of your payment to the insurance company. Again, these things must be decided prior to the annuitization of your contract. Except in very rare cases, once this begins, you cannot change how you receive your money.

Maximizing Your Annuity's Distributions

Now comes the fun part. You have retired and are ready to start living your dream. Now what? You will need money to fund this distribution, while also providing for your long-term needs.

Retirement Planning: This is what you have been waiting for. You have been planning all your life for this, and now you want to maximize what you have. Forming a budget will be of great use at this stage. It will allow you to know exactly how much money you need and when every month.

You might be saving for a dream purchase or vacation; whatever your financial goals are, an annuity will give you a source of income.

Long-term Care or Life Insurance: Many times, annuities are used to fund other types of insurance, such as long-term care or life insurance. On average, one out of every two people will need some sort of long-term care, whether they stay in their home or move into a skilled nursing facility. Annuities can be perfect for funding this type of insurance, assuming you have enough expendable income to live on.

Rather than using one to fund the other, thanks to the Pension Protection Act of 2006, long-term care insurance and annuities combined into a single product in 2010. This should be cheaper than buying the two insurance products separately. These products are still in development stages, though, and may not be immediately available in all states.

Who Gets the Money?

It is important to note that in owner-driven annuities, when the annuitant dies, no payments to the annuitant's beneficiaries occur. Because the contract is owner-driven, if, and only if, the owner dies does the beneficiary receive a death benefit.

In annuitant-driven contracts, this is not the case. Because the annuitant has control of the contract, his or her beneficiary will receive the funds in the event of his or her death.

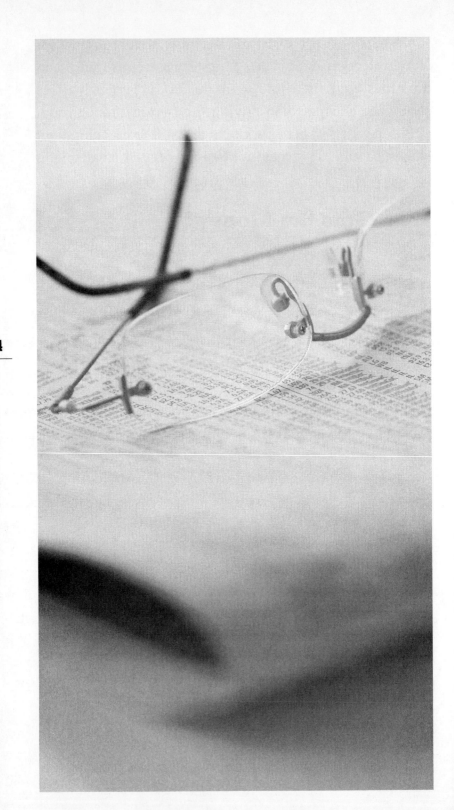

Chapter 17

The Future of Annuities

Annuities have seen great changes over the years. Founded during the ancient Roman era, annuities have gone from mere life-long streams of payment — known as annua — to sophisticated investment products. They grew in popularity once again in Europe in the 1600s. It is said that even Shakespeare, toward the end of his life, purchased an annuity.

In the U.S., annuities are not new either. The first group annuities were sold in 1759 to ministers in Pennsylvania. Individual annuities later became available in 1912, again in Pennsylvania, from the Pennsylvania Company for Insurance on Lives and Granting Annuities. During the 1930s, annuities took on a new popularity because many were worried about the financial health of the stock market. During the Great Depression, annuities and insurance products were still considered safe investments. Even then, annuities were tax-deferred.

Variable annuities are relatively new on the scene. The first variable annuities were sold in 1952 and correlated with the advent of mutual funds. By some estimates, there are twice as many mutual funds as stocks available in the U.S. market. The individuals managing those funds made some subaccounts available to insurance companies, thus the creation of variable annuities. Although variable annuities may be more recent, they have certainly become the most popular because of their potential for great and safe earnings.

Annuities will continue to evolve, especially because people are living longer. As life expectancies continue to rise, annuities will adapt to meet the needs of the population. Although the investment vehicle continually changes, the most important basic feature of annuities has remained intact; they are still tax-deferred investments. And, with more than $200 billion spent each year in annuity sales, the popularity of annuities, both fixed and variable, looks like it will continue to increase, especially as the baby boomer generation reaches retirement age.

Rates

As the economy fluctuates, investors will be looking for the most competitive rates. In poor market times, the guarantees that fixed annuities offer appear attractive. The stock market, though, has grown at a steady pace since the Great Depression, with the exception of a few ups and downs. In order to keep up, fixed annuities will need to offer more enticing rates. Fixed annuities will need to offer at least a few points higher than the historical rate of inflation: 3 percent. With low rates, there is no incentive for investors to choose fixed annuities, especially because CDs also offer low rates, and the money is not locked up for as long within a CD as it would be inside an annuity. CDs offer more liquidity than fixed annuities because of the fact that the average CD is accessible after only one year. With comparable low rates, many investors would opt for the CD so their money is more accessible.

Budgeting requires consistency of income. Retirees are far more likely to set a budget for themselves because they are on a limited income. Variable annuities, under current practices, are, for the most part, inconsistent. Fluctuations in income need to be addressed by insurance companies. One way to do this is through a floor guarantee, which some annuities already offer. More companies are finding that this brings more business to their variable annuities because they guarantee payments will never fall less than a certain percentage of the first distribution. If there is an 80 percent floor and the first monthly distribution received is for $1,000, the investor will never receive less than $800 per month. This trend will most likely continue because it has seen much success.

Accessibility

Immediate annuities have a large downfall — their accessibility. As more people put money into annuities, there will most likely be more demand that they can withdraw money when and as they need it. Traditional immediate annuities, although guaranteeing a source of income for life, have very little liquidity. If there was easier access to these monies, retirees would be far more likely to invest their money in them. Insurance companies may find that if they changed the accessibility policies concerning immediate annuities, they would generate more business.

3 Methods of gaining accessibility to your annuity money

1. **Annuitization early.**

   If you exercise your contract early, you will start receiving monthly distributions. This option works well if you do not need a large sum of money immediately. Once you annuitize your contract, it is impossible, unless you sell your contract on the secondary market — see point 3 — to gain access to the entire sum of your investment. You will receive your monthly distributions

2. **Terminate the contract.**

   If you have not held your annuity for long, you will have a penalty to pay, but you will receive your money quickly. Penalties are determined by the length of time you have held the contract. As time progresses, penalties will decline. A typical penalty is 10 percent if you cancel your contract within the first year. Each successive year of a ten-year surrender period will see a drop of a percentage point until zero is reached. These fees are meant to encourage investors to keep their money within the annuity and thus, within the possession of the insurance company.

3. **Sell your annuity in the secondary market.**

   This is perhaps the least profitable of these choices, but if you have already begun the annuitization process and an emergency arises, this might be your only choice. Taking a little time to shop around for the best offer may save you thousands of dollars.

Preferential Treatment

The wealthy are prone to ignoring annuities, even though they may be the people who would profit from them the most. With preferential treatment of higher income customers, insurance companies would see a huge increase in business. Upper-class investors oftentimes think of themselves as self-insured and thus, not needing any insurance products. If insurance companies were to raise rates for those who deposited $1 million or more, this outlook would probably change. Offering higher rates to those who put more in their accounts may seem like a loss at first because insurance companies would have to pay out more, but with proper money management techniques, the insurance companies would have more revenue to invest in their private holdings, generating higher profits for themselves, as well as for their clients.

Another way clients might achieve preferred status is by holding more than one policy with the same company. If an individual purchases a life insurance policy from a company, that company could include a bonus or a reduced charge for signing an annuity contract as well. This would encourage clients to stay with the company they are most familiar with.

Living Benefits

Guaranteed **living benefits** are just starting to gain popularity among investors. This trend will most likely continue far into the future, especially if the market remains uncertain. It is likely people will soon see the cost of living benefits decrease, possibly to zero, so that more investors will take advantage of them. Rather than having a fee associated with them, living benefits may require a longer surrender period. In short, with more living benefits being added to annuity options, it makes picking and customizing the annuity that each investor needs that much easier. Living benefits minimize the risk assumed by the annuitant and instead place the onus upon the insurance companies.

Taxation

It is not likely that the methods of taxation regarding annuities will change in the future. Tax deferral was instituted to encourage people to save for retirement with the hope that more people would not be dependent on government welfare programs. The capital gains tax, however, is set to increase. This would have a huge impact on annuities, which are taxed as income, and not capital gains. As people shift their money from mutual funds and other market-sensitive products to annuities, annuities will probably grow in popularity because they will avoid the capital gains tax.

Another proposed tax break relates directly to immediate income annuities. This proposal would lower the tax rate on immediate annuities to a rate lower than the investor's normal rate of income tax but higher than the capital gains rate. This is by no means guaranteed to happen, as it is still in the early stages of discussion within the governmental structure.

Also, favorable to individuals shopping for an annuity is the fact that there is some talk of making tax laws for annuities more favorable. The proposed legislation is probably still some years in the making but would make a certain percentage of annuity investment dollars tax exempt. This would not be a huge leap; IRAs are currently treated in a similar manner, making them very popular among younger investors. Annuities would certainly be more attractive to the same clientele.

Longevity

People are living longer than ever. If the average life expectancy were to increase by ten years, insurance companies would have to restructure their payouts in order to account for this dramatic change or else face big trouble. This concept is already taken into account with the differences between the sexes, and the fact that women, on average, live five years longer than men so they receive less money per month from their annuities with the distribution difference being made up by their added life expectancy.

Social Security

As more baby boomers reach retirement age, fewer people are left populating the workforce. This leaves fewer people who are paying Social Security taxes for a larger number of people receiving the money. In short, the status of Social Security 50 years from now is unknown. Some experts believe it will survive indefinitely, while others question its lasting power. Either way, people need to be prepared. Social Security is essentially a government-sponsored annuity — individuals pay into it their entire working lives and then see the benefits once they retire. If Social Security becomes privatized, as some believe it will, people need to be prepared and invest accordingly. In short, no one can predict the future, and because of this, preparation is necessary.

Here's an example: An individual turns 65 in 2014, and he earned $50,000 per year at the time of retirement. According to the calculator at **www.ssa.gov/retire2/AnypiaApplet.html**, he would roughly earn $1,452.00 per month in benefits. If Social Security benefits were to disappear or be reduced, that would be a large blow to his finances. An alternative safety net needs to be instituted. Annuities, when properly used, can be that safety net.

Technology

The Internet has done wonders for investors. Rather than pouring over newspapers and books, any information that could be desired is at an investor's fingertips. This phenomenon has even affected annuities. The research process has been condensed for would-be investors. Sites like **www.annuityadvantage.com** compare and contrast annuities from all over the country, making it extremely easy to research the products out there. This site not only compare rates and the strengths of the insurance companies featured, but it does so all in one place, making it easier for investors to see the differences. *See Appendix B for a checklist of the key points for comparison between annuities.*

As society becomes more technologically savvy, there will be more investment options online. Already it is possible to set up the purchase of annuities online through some insurance companies like Allianz. Researching different products and reallocating assets has become a much simpler task as well. This trend will definitely continue on into the future.

Another way in which the Internet has helped is with people wishing to get out of their annuity contracts. There are many sites out there that offer to buy your annuity; a simple Web search will reveal dozens of companies that hunger for your annuity. It must be stressed again that this should only be done as a last resort. Your annuity is worth much more over the long run than the price these companies will give you right away.

Conclusion

This book aims to shed light onto an often confusing subject. There is a lot of information out there concerning the subject of annuities, and not all of it is easily understood. Hopefully, with the insight given here, you will be able to properly fund a long and enjoyable retirement, which is probably what you have worked for all of these years.

Although there is no silver bullet annuity that will solve each and every individual's needs, there is certainly an annuity out there for everyone. Each person's situation is unique and should be treated as such. With that in mind, there are a few key lessons that should be emphasized.

Have a clear-cut goal. What is your reasoning for purchasing the annuity? The answer to this question will help you to determine the type of annuity that will work best for you. It will also help you determine which riders will apply toward achieving your goals.

Put it in writing. By putting the goal you come up with in writing, you will help hold yourself accountable for achieving that goal.

Do not invest money you will need in the short-term.
There are hefty penalties for withdrawing too much money too quickly because annuities are not meant as short-term investments. Cash accounts like savings and money market accounts where funds have more liquidity are much better suited for the short term.

Make sure your paperwork is up to date. There are many pitfalls you can fall into if you are not vigilant regarding the logistics of an annuity. If your beneficiary passes away before you do or if you have an ex-spouse named as a beneficiary, it will only take a few minutes to correct this. Make sure your money goes where you intend it to go.

Shop around. There are thousands of annuities out there; you just need to look around to find them. The resources within this book are a good start. A few phone calls to local insurance agencies will also be beneficial.

Ask questions. Annuities can be confusing, but it is a necessity that you understand the investment you are making. The questions included in this book are a good starting point, but there may be other questions that pertain to your situation. Remember that there is no such thing as a bad question; this is especially true when it comes to your money.

Diversify your portfolio. The more spread out your variable annuity is, the safer the money will be against short-term losses. By properly allocating your funds, you will avoid the majority of short-term losses.

Monitor your subaccounts. This can be as simple as a quick look online at your account each month. There are also some annuities out there that will manage your allocation for you. If the idea of managing your own funds frightens you, these annuities are not for you.

Be aware of the fees associated with your annuity. There is no point in paying extra for something you do not want. There is also no point in paying a high fee for an annuity when the same deal may be available at a lesser cost.

Be aware of any taxes involved. There is no way to avoid taxes, but annuities, especially qualified annuities, come pretty close. Be aware of what tax bracket you fall under and how contributions to an annuity will help relieve rather than increase your tax burden.

These highlights summarize a very broad subject; by no means is this list all-inclusive; however, it highlights the key steps you should take in purchasing and owning an annuity. Regardless of which type of annuity or annuities you ultimately select to fund your dream retirement, you will need to take these points into consideration. Remember, it is your money — you deserve to have the retirement you always wished for.

Appendix A

Guaranty Associations

In order to sell insurance products, companies must belong to their state's Guaranty Association. It is in violation of the law for an insurance company to advertise that it belongs to the Guaranty Association because of the fact that the relationship between the two entities could be misconstrued by potential customers, giving the companies that advertise as belonging to this Association an unfair advantage in gaining clients. The National Organization of Life and Health Insurance Guaranty Associations oversees each state's particular Association. Their site can be found at **www.nolhga.com**.

Each state has a particular amount guaranteed to investors in case the insurance company they have invested their money in fails. The amounts given are all for current cash value unless otherwise stipulated. The following chart is current as of the end of 2009.

| Alabama | $300,000 in current value, $100,000 in surrender value. |
| Alaska | $100,000. |

Arizona	$100,000.
Arkansas	$300,000.
California	80 percent of the present value, up to a $100,000 maximum.
Colorado	$100,000, including present value and surrender value.
Connecticut	$500,000.
Delaware	$100,000.
Florida	$300,000 in present value, $100,000 in surrender value.
Georgia	$300,000 in present value, $100,000 in surrender value.
Hawaii	$100,000.
Idaho	$250,000 in cash surrender or withdrawal value.
Illinois	$100,000 per annuitant, including surrender value.
Indiana	$100,000.
Iowa	$250,000, including cash value.
Kansas	$100,000.
Kentucky	$100,000, including cash value.
Louisiana	$250,000.
Maine	$250,000, including surrender and cash value.

Maryland	$100,000, including surrender and cash value.
Massachusetts	$100,000.
Michigan	$250,000 in qualified accounts, such as 403(b), IRA, and Roth IRA annuities, $100,000 in all nonqualified accounts.
Minnesota	$250,000 in surrender value, $410,000 in present value if there is a period certain of ten years (or more) to life.
Mississippi	$100,000.
Missouri	$100,000.
Montana	$100,000.
Nebraska	$100,000.
Nevada	$100,000.
New Hampshire	$100,000.
New Jersey	$500,000 in current value, $100,000 in surrender value.
New Mexico	$100,000 cash or surrender value.
New York	$500,000.
North Carolina	$300,000.
North Dakota	$100,000.
Ohio	$100,000.
Oklahoma	$300,000.

Oregon	$100,000.
Pennsylvania	$300,000 in annuity value, including $100,000 in cash value.
Rhode Island	$100,000.
South Carolina	$300,000 aggregate.
South Dakota	$100,000 per contract owner.
Tennessee	$250,000.
Texas	$100,000 per annuitant.
Utah	$200,000.
Vermont	$250,000.
Virginia	$100,000.
Washington	$500,000.
West Virginia	$100,000.
Wisconsin	$300,000.
Wyoming	$100,000 total, including cash and surrender value.

Appendix B

Resources

The following websites have been consulted in the writing of this book and have proven they will be of use to you, the investor, as well. The list includes insurance companies, rating organizations, online comparison sites, annuity calculators, and government resources.

RESOURCE	LINK
A.M. Best	www.ambest.com
Allianz	www.allianz.com
American Family Life Assurance Company of Columbus	www.aflac.com
Annuity Advantage	www.annuityadvantage.com
AnnuityFYI	www.annuityfyi.com
Bankers Life and Casualty	www.bankers.com
Guaranty Income Life Insurance Company	www.gilico.com
Immediate Annuities	www.immediateannuities.com
Internal Revenue Service	www.irs.gov
Investopedia	www.investopedia.com
KJE Computer Solutions	http://www.dinkytown.net/

MassMutual	www.massmutual.com
Moody's Investors Service	www.moodys.com
Morningstar	www.morningstar.com
National Clearinghouse for Long-Term Care Information	www.longtermcare.gov
National Organization of Life & Health Insurance Guaranty Associations	www.nolhga.com
New York Stock Exchange	www.nyse.com
Peach Tree Settlement Funding	www.peachtreefinancial.com
Prudential	www.prudential.com
Standard & Poor's	www.standardandpoors.com
State Farm Insurance	www.statefarm.com
Steele Financial Solutions	www.steelefinancialsolutions.com/
T. Rowe Price	www.troweprice.com
TIAA-CREF	www.tiaa-cref.org
U.S. Department of Labor	http://data.bls.gov/cgi-bin/cpicalc.pl
U.S. Securities and Exchange Commission	www.sec.gov
U.S. Social Security Administration	www.ssa.gov
Vanguard	www.vanguard.com
Yahoo! Finance	http://finance.yahoo.com

The Complete Guide to Investing in Annuities

Appendix C

Getting the Investment Help You Need

There are many resources out there that will help guide you through the world of investing. Although this book touches upon many key points, it is always helpful to refer to other sources so you find exactly what will help you most.

The following sites are dedicated to helping out investors not only with fixed and variable annuities but also with all types of investments. Although an annuity plays a vital role in the vast majority of retirement portfolios, they should seldom be used as the sole funding source for a retirement, especially by younger investors.

Not each of these sites will have all of the information you are looking for, but if you do decide that an annuity alone will not cover all of your needs, with a little research, you will find what you are looking for.

Advisory Newsletter: A publication that provides market commentary and investment recommendations. Most advisory newsletters are subscription services. *See Hulbert Financial Digest.*

American Association of Individual Investors (AAII): A networking and education organization for individual investors. On the web at **www.aaii.com**.

Barron's: A weekly finance magazine published by Dow Jones, Inc. It is available in print format or an online subscription. It is available online at **www.barrons.com**.

Bond Buyer, The: A daily publication for the bond market that contains a comprehensive listing of municipal bond data. *The Bond Buyer* was established in 1891 and is also known as *The Daily Bond Buyer*. On the web at **www.bondbuyer.com**.

Bond Market Association (BMA): A trade association comprised of banks, dealers, brokers, and underwriters of debt instruments. The BMA also provides educational services to individual investors. On the web at **www.bondmarkets.com**.

Certified Fund Specialist: A financial professional who possesses a certificate attesting to his or her qualification to advising clients on the selection of mutual fund investments.

Commodity Trading Adviser: A person who is registered with the Commodity Futures Trading Commission (CFTC) to provide, advise, and manage futures and options trading activity for another person.

Compustat: A subscription service from Standard & Poor's that provides market information and fundamental data.

Dun & Bradstreet (D&B): A business and research company that issues corporate credit ratings and maintains a database of financial information on corporations worldwide. A company's D&B rating can affect both its stock price and its bond rating. On the web at **www.dnb.com**.

EDGAR Online: A publicly traded company that provides value-added data services based on the Securities and Exchange Commission's EDGAR database of corporate filings. EDGAR Online trades under the symbol EDGR on NASDAQ and is online at **www.edgar-online.com**.

Federal Register: A government publication that provides public notice of new regulations from the Office of Thrift Supervision, legal notices, presidential proclamations, executive orders, documents required by an Act of Congress, and other official documents of public interest. The Federal Register is published daily, Monday through Friday, and is available on the web at **www.gpoaccess.gov/fr/index.html**.

Fitch Investors Service: The company that issues the Fitch Ratings for the bond, Eurobond, and funds market. Compare to Moody's Investor Service and Standard & Poor's.

Hulbert Financial Digest: A MarketWatch/Dow Jones subscription service that rates advisory newsletters by tracking and measuring their recommendations against actual performance. The digest is available by e-mail or

U.S. Postal Service delivery. On the web at **www.market-watch.com**.

Investment Advisor Registration Depository: A NASD-developed and operated system that maintains registration and disclosure information on registered investment advisers. On the web at **www.iard.com**.

Investment Adviser: A professional hired by an individual to provide financial and investment advice.

Investor Protection Trust: A nonprofit organization that provides resources to help individual investors make informed investment decisions. On the web at **www.investorprotection.org**.

Investors Business Daily (IBD): A daily financial newspaper and Internet-based investment news and information resource. On the web at **www.investors.com**.

Moody's Investors Service: A financial research firm opining on the creditworthiness of bond issuers. On the web at **www.moodys.com**.

Morningstar, Inc.: An investment research and rating service for mutual funds, stocks, closed-end funds, exchange traded funds, hedge funds, and other investments. On the web at **www.morningstar.com**.

National Association of Investors Corporation (NAIC): A networking and educational resource for individual investors.

Reuters: A global business and financial news service. In addition to news content for media organizations, Reuters provides financial information products to businesses, financial professionals, and investors. On the web at **www.reuters.com**.

Standard & Poor's: A market research firm that publishes credit ratings and financial reports used by individuals and institutional investors. It is also the originator of the S&P indices, the best known and most closely watched of which is the S&P 500. On the web at **www.standardandpoors.com**.

Value Line, Inc.: An investment research firm with product offerings for individual, professional, and institutional investors. Value Line is known for the Value Line Investment Survey for stock analysis, but the company has similar products for mutual funds and options as well. On the web at **www.valueline.com**.

Wall Street Journal, The: A financial news publication from Dow Jones and Company. It is available in print daily and online. On the web at **www.wsj.com**.

Appendix D

The Importance of Interest Compounding

Interest compounding is a beautiful thing, and the sooner you can start investing, the better funded your retirement will be. The example on the following pages shows two different investors over a 45-year period. The investor in Example 1 only invested for 8 out of the 47 years, while Example 2's investor contributed for 39 years. Although the Example 1 investor donated far less, because he did so early in his life, interest compounding had a huge effect on how his investment played out. This chart assumes a 10 percent rate of return each year.

EXAMPLE 1		EXAMPLE 2	
Annual Investment	Year-End Value	Annual Investment	Year-End Value
$2,000	$2,200	$0	$0
$2,000	$4,620	$0	$0
$2,000	$7,282	$0	$0
$2,000	$10,210	$0	$0
$2,000	$13,431	$0	$0
$2,000	$16,974	$0	$0
$2,000	$20,872	$0	$0
$2,000	$25,159	$0	$0
$0	$27,675	$2,000	$2,200

EXAMPLE 1		EXAMPLE 2	
Annual Investment	Year-End Value	Annual Investment	Year-End Value
$0	$30,442	$2,000	$4,620
$0	$33,487	$2,000	$7,282
$0	$36,835	$2,000	$10,210
$0	$40,519	$2,000	$13,431
$0	$44,571	$2,000	$16,974
$0	$49,028	$2,000	$20,872
$0	$53,931	$2,000	$25,159
$0	$59,324	$2,000	$29,875
$0	$65,256	$2,000	$35,062
$0	$71,782	$2,000	$40,769
$0	$78,960	$2,000	$47,045
$0	$86,856	$2,000	$53,950
$0	$95,541	$2,000	$61,545
$0	$105,095	$2,000	$69,899
$0	$115,605	$2,000	$79,089
$0	$127,165	$2,000	$89,198
$0	$139,882	$2,000	$100,318
$0	$153,870	$2,000	$112,550
$0	$169,257	$2,000	$126,005
$0	$186,183	$2,000	$140,805
$0	$204,801	$2,000	$157,086
$0	$225,281	$2,000	$174,995
$0	$247,809	$2,000	$194,694
$0	$272,590	$2,000	$216,364
$0	$299,849	$2,000	$240,200
$0	$329,834	$2,000	$266,420
$0	$362,818	$2,000	$295,262
$0	$399,100	$2,000	$326,988
$0	$439,010	$2,000	$361,887
$0	$482,910	$2,000	$400,276
$0	$531,202	$2,000	$442,503

EXAMPLE 1		EXAMPLE 2	
Annual Investment	Year-End Value	Annual Investment	Year-End Value
$0	$584,322	$2,000	$488,953
$0	$642,754	$2,000	$540,049
$0	$707,029	$2,000	$596,254
$0	$777,732	$2,000	$658,079
$0	$855,505	$2,000	$726,087
$0	$941,056	$2,000	$800,896
$0	$1,035,161	$2,000	$883,185

This example is an extreme, but it proves a point. Interest compounding will do far more for you than just additional premiums will. Over the 47-year period, the first investor only added $16,000 to his account, but because they were the first eight years, he was able to multiply his nest egg to more than $1 million. The second investor contributed $78,000 to her account and multiplied her nest egg to more than $800,000. Which investor would you rather be?

Glossary

401(k): A tax-deferred retirement investment set up through an employer.

Accumulation Period: The period in which the owner of the annuity deposits money into the account.

Advanced Life Deferred Annuity: An annuity geared toward guaranteeing that an individual will never run out of money no matter what age he or she lives to. These annuities do not start distributions until the annuitant reaches age 80 or 85.

Agent: The company representative who sells insurance products.

Annual Reset: A method of applying interest to an equity-indexed annuity that looks at the beginning and ending amounts of the selected index during the course of a year. The amount credited to the annuity is contingent on how the index performed.

Annuitant: The individual who receives distributions from the annuity contract once the annuitization period begins.

Annuitization Period: The period where the money invested into the annuity is returned to the individual investor.

Annuity: A contract between an individual and an insurance company where the individual entrusts an amount of money to the insurance company.

Arbitrage: The act of buying in one market and then immediately reselling for a higher price in a second market. This also refers to the purchase of a life insurance policy when the insured passes away and an heir receives a greater amount of money than was put into the policy.

Asset Allocation: The practice of dividing capital between a number of different risk classes. This can be done within one investment, such as a variable annuity, or among several types of investments.

Assumed Interest Rate: The rate chosen by an investor before distributions on an immediate variable annuity begins. The first several distributions are given using this chosen interest rate until the true earnings of the annuity take over.

Averaging: The portfolio averaging method of crediting interest looks at the company's investments as a whole. If the company is going to apply 5 percent to its annuities, the entire balance of the annuity would be credited with 5 percent.

Banding: The practice of applying interest separately to each year's contributions. For example, the $1,000 invested in year one of the annuity may be accruing interest at 5 percent, while the $1,000 invested in year two may only be accruing interest at 4.5 percent.

Beneficiary: In the event that the annuitant dies, the beneficiary receives all eligible funds left over.

Bonus: An artificially high interest rate meant to attract clients. The interest rate is only good for the first year of the contract before going back to the normal interest rate.

Broker: A representative of a company that sells insurance products. Brokers normally have access to variable products.

Capital: Liquid assets, such as cash.

Capital Gains: Income not directly related to employment. This can be realized as a gain in stock prices, an inheritance, or a gift.

Cap Rate: The maximum rate of return that a contract will be given.

CD-Type Annuities: An annuity that offers rates competitive with certificates of deposit. These annuities are kept for short periods, typically 5 to 10 years, and have large penalties for early withdrawal.

Certificate of Deposit: A contract between an individual and a bank where the investor is guaranteed a specified rate of return in exchange for his or her investment.

Commission: The amount an insurance agent receives in return for selling an annuity or other insurance product. This is a percentage of the premium paid by the client.

Compound Interest: A method of crediting interest to an account where the principal amount earns interest, as well as any interest that has already been applied to the investment.

Contingent-Deferred Sales Charge: A penalty added to an annuity's cost if the annuity is liquidated during the surrender period. This can account for as much as 8 to 10 percent of the total value of the annuity.

Death Benefit: The amount of money an heir would receive from an insurance or annuity contract in the event of the owner's death.

Dividends: The practice of sharing profits directly with stock holders. Rather than seeing an increase in the price of a stock, dividends are distributed on a yearly basis directly to stock holders. If a variable annuity includes individual stocks, dividends are generally not given to the annuity owner.

Dollar Cost Averaging: The practice of investing the same amount into a subaccount regularly over a period so the annuitant gets more shares when they are cheap and fewer when they are expensive. This method can have great results if done over a long period.

Equity-indexed Annuity: A type of fixed annuity that is dependent on a market index. Rather than sharing in both the losses and profits of that index, equity-indexed annuities have a set interest rate they will not fall below. Likewise, if the index increases in price, the annuity will not increase as much as a variable annuity would.

Exchange: A Section 1035 exchange refers to the tax-free exchange of one insurance product for another. Annuities that have not yet been annuitized can be exchanged with other annuities in order to get higher rates of return.

Exchange Traded Funds: A basket of like stocks grouped together in a single investment. These are technically considered to be mutual funds, although they are not overseen by a fund manager.

Exclusion Ratio: The mathematical formula that determines what percentage of the annuity profits are given to the government for taxes.

Expense Planning: The process of calculating how much money you will need to maintain your desired standard of living during your retirement years. This can be calculated as a monthly or yearly amount.

First in, First Out: The practice of taking non-taxable dollars out of an annuity first, leaving the taxable amount left within the fund so no taxes are paid on the annuity for the first several distributions. This practice is only applicable to annuities purchased prior to Aug. 14, 1982.

Fixed Annuities: An annuity that promises a set rate of return for a specific amount of time. After the set time is over, the insurance company may choose to alter the fixed rate but must notify annuitants.

Flexible Premium: A premium that can be changed by the owner from year to year, or month to month.

Floating Rates: A type of fixed annuity that may vary its rates from month to month.

Floor on Interest: A method of controlling interest rates in equity-indexed annuities. The most common floor is 0 percent; a guarantee that the annuity will not lose money even when the market is in a downtrend.

Free Look Period: The amount of time between the policy delivery and when the annuitant can cancel the policy without incurring a penalty from the insurance company. In most states, the free look period is 30 days.

High-Water Mark: The method of applying interest to an annuity that looks at the highest point in the market during a given cycle. This rate is then applied to the entire annuity as its rate of return for the given period.

Home Equity Conversion Mortgage: *See Reverse Mortgage.*

Immediate Annuity: Also called an income annuity, immediate annuities provide a stream of income within the first year of the purchase of the contract. This annuity is funded by a single lump-sum premium.

Impaired Risk Annuity: An annuity purchased for a high-risk individual. Because high-risk individuals have shorter life expectancies, these annuities generally have higher monthly distributions.

Income Annuity: *See Immediate Annuity.*

Index: A group of stocks that acts as a measure for a particular sector of the market.

Index Option: The right, but not the requisite, to purchase or sell shares of an index for a set price at a later date. *See Option for more detail.*

Individual Retirement Account: A tax-deferred retirement account for an individual that permits individuals to set aside money each year, with earnings tax-deferred until withdrawals begin at age 59½ or later (or earlier, with a 10% penalty).

Interest Capping: A method of accruing interest on an account stating that no matter how well the market performs in a given cycle, the interest applied to the annuity will not go higher than a certain percentage.

Interest Compounding: The practice of allowing the interest gained in an account to gain its own interest.

Joint and 100 Percent Survivor: This is a payment option that allows a surviving spouse, or another beneficiary, to have access to 100 percent of the annuity's funds after the original annuitant has passed away.

Large Cap Stocks: These are businesses that see the highest amount of trading in their company stock. They are considered to be safer investments than smaller, lesser-known and lesser-traded companies.

Last in, First out: The process of taxing the gains of an account upon withdrawal. This is how current annuities are taxed.

Law of Large Numbers: A mathematical theory stating that the larger the sample, the closer the statistics of the sample will be to the general population.

Liquidate: The act of cashing in an account in order to receive cash.

Liquidity: The accessibility of funds in an account. The more accessible the funds, the higher the degree of liquidity.

Living Benefits: The perks of owning an annuity that are experienced while the annuitant is still alive.

Long Term Care Insurance: An insurance policy that will cover all or a portion of the costs associated with a long-term care stay. Some policies also have home health care riders.

Look-Back: A method of crediting interest to equity-indexed annuities that literally reviews the past year and selects the highest point that the appropriate index was at before applying the increase to the annuity.

Low-Water Mark: A method of crediting interest which looks at the lowest point in the market during a review period.

Margin Fees: The difference between the rate actually earned by the index that a variable annuity is tracking and the amount credited to the annuity.

Market Index: A group of stocks bunched together to gauge the overall strength of the market. The Dow Jones Industrial Average is a famous example.

Market Value Adjustment: Found in some fixed annuities, this feature will adjust the value of each withdrawal in terms of how the interest rates have been performing. If rates go up, the value of withdrawals will go down; if rates sink, withdrawals will go up.

Maturity Date: The date on which an investor can withdraw from his or her annuity without incurring surrender period fees. This can also refer to the date on which a bond can be redeemed for full profits.

Minimum Interest Rate: The lowest rate that an insurance company will offer on an annuity. This rate will be stipulated in the contract.

Money Laundering: The act of concealing the source of illegally obtained money.

Mortality and Expense Risk Fee: A major source of profit for insurance companies. This yearly fee is oftentimes presented as a percentage of the capital held within the annuity account. These fees can be as high as 2 percent in some cases.

Mutual Fund: An investment vehicle that pools together many investors' capital in order to fulfill the purpose set forth by the fund's manager. All holdings and strategies are detailed in the prospectus.

Nonqualified Plans: An annuity purchased with dollars that have already been taxed.

Option: The choice to buy or sell a stock or commodity at an agreed upon price sometime in the future. Options are not mandatory, but you will lose the option fee if you choose not to act upon your right.

Owner: The individual who signs the contract and supplies the premiums paid to the insurance company.

Participation Rate: The percentage of profits that an equity-indexed annuity credits to accounts when an index increases in price. For example, if the participation rate is 80 percent, if the index rises 10 percent, the equity-indexed annuity will rise 8 percent.

Penalty-free Withdrawals: A withdrawal from an annuity that avoids the surrender period fee. Usually, you can withdraw up to 10 percent of your annuity's balance without incurring the surrender period penalty.

Pension: An employer-sponsored retirement plan that consists of company stock.

Point-to-Point: A method of crediting interest to an annuity that looks at the entire surrender period before applying any profits to the annuity's balance.

Portfolio Average: A method of crediting interest to an annuity that looks at the entire portfolio of the insurance company's holdings prior to applying any losses or profits to an individual account.

Position: Buying or selling a security or commodity.

Premium: A payment for an insurance policy.

Principal: The amount of money put into an account. The principal does not include any interest gained.

Probate: A court procedure meant to bring closure to the estate of a deceased.

Prospectus: The paper brochure that lists each of the sub-accounts and how they have performed historically.

Qualified Plans: An annuity that is purchased with dollars that have not yet been taxed.

Renewal Rate: The rate of return issued on an annuity after the rate of return for the first year of the contract has expired.

Reverse Mortgage: A loan taken out against the value of a home. The amount borrowed plus interest accrued will not exceed the value of the home over the entirety of the loan. This type of loan does not need to be repaid until the home is sold or the borrower dies.

Rider: A rider is an add-on to a policy. There may or may not be a fee associated with riders.

Risk Class: This refers to the amount of risk an investment takes. Normally, higher risk classes are more volatile, meaning you may see more losses, but there is also the potential for bigger gains.

Section 1035: Found in the U.S. Internal Revenue Code, Section 1035 is where exchanges between insurance products are discussed. A proper 1035 exchange is non-taxable.

Self-insuring: The process of saving enough wealth so you can support yourself and your family without the use of annuities or other insurance products.

Series 6: An exam an insurance agent must pass in order to be eligible to sell variable insurance products.

Simple Interest: An alternative to compounding interest, simple interest only credits the principal amount in an investment. Interest credited will not earn its own interest.

Small Cap Stocks: These are smaller companies that do not see much trading with their company stock. They are subject to greater fluctuation because big trades can cause bigger swings in stock price.

Social Security: A government mandated pension fund. Each U.S. citizen contributes in the form of taxes taken out of their paycheck. When someone becomes disabled or retires, he or she can begin receiving funds back.

Solvency: An insurance company's ability to pay insured individuals the money they are owed. A solvent company has enough liquid assets to pay any claims at a given point in time.

Split Annuity: A combination of a single premium immediate annuity and a fixed deferred annuity which practically guarantees you a steady source of income for life.

Spread Fees: *See Margin Fees.*

Staging: The process of buying annuities at different times so they mature at different points in an annuitants life.

Stock Market: The place where stocks are bought and sold. This can mean either the physical place where trading occurs or the universal act of the buying and selling of stocks.

Subaccount: A smaller account within an annuity that is controlled by a funds manager. Each subaccount has a goal, such as growth or income.

Suitability: The insurance professional's term for determining which product is best for an investor. This is the process of selecting the annuity that best suits the investor.

Surrender Period: The period during which you may liquidate your annuity and receive funds back minus a penalty. Typical surrender periods decrease in penalty percentage for the first several years until the penalty reaches 0 percent.

Survivorship Credits: A concept closely related to mortality pooling. Survivorship credits are the profits that annuitants gain from other annuities whose annuitants have died prior to collecting their full share of distributions.

Tax Deferral: The act of not paying taxes on an investment until withdrawals begin. Annuities grow tax-deferred.

Tax-sheltered Annuity: Defined in the Internal Revenue Code Section 403(b), a tax-sheltered annuity is a retirement account designed especially for individuals working in the nonprofit sector.

Three-Tier System: A classic retirement funding strategy involving the holding of cash accounts, corporate bonds, and stocks.

Trader: Someone who buys and sells securities for short-term profits.

Underwriting: The internal process an insurance policy goes through before being approved by the insurance company. This will require a doctor's record of health for the proposed insured.

Variable Annuity: An annuity that is somehow connected to the stock market, thus making its returns variable depending on the market's performance.

Vesting: The amount of time you must keep your money in an account before earnings are applied.

Bibliography

Dellinger, Jeffrey K. *The Handbook of Variable Income Annuities.* John Wiley & Sons, Inc.: New York, 2006.

Huggard, John P. *Investing With Variable Annuities: Fifty Reasons Why Variables Annuities May Be Better Long-Term Investments Than Mutual Funds.* Parker-Thompson Publishing: Raleigh, NC, 2002.

Pechter, Kerry. *Annuities for Dummies.* Wiley Publishing, Inc.: Indianapolis, 2008.

Williamson, Gordon K. *Getting Started in Annuities.* John Wiley & Sons, Inc.: New York, 1999.

About the Author

Matthew Young is a New York State licensed life, accident, and health insurance agent. He lives in Upstate New York with his family. Young currently works as a paralegal for a real estate law firm.

Index

The Complete Guide to Investing in Annuities

R

Reinsurance, 33-36

Renewal rate, 76, 79, 277

Risk class, 30, 95, 98, 102, 107, 143, 277

Risk reduction, 103

Risk tolerance, 44, 87, 93-94, 104

S

Self-insuring, 38, 43, 54, 98, 277

Social Security, 20, 22, 41-43, 51, 59, 67, 78, 162-164, 167, 181, 209, 221, 231, 241-242, 254, 278

Standard & Poor's, 16, 24, 111, 186-187, 254, 257, 259

State guaranty funds, 33

Stock market, 14-15, 17, 23-24, 27, 31-33, 43-45, 49, 53, 55, 67, 73-74, 82, 87, 90, 92-93, 95, 106, 121, 123, 180, 235-236, 279-280

Straight life annuities, 63, 66, 70, 194

Surrender fees, 108, 172, 211, 274

T

Tax bracket, 18-19, 21, 51-52, 96, 127, 150-152, 155, 159, 172, 179-181, 195, 247

Tax exempt, 241

Tax-sheltered annuities, 30, 125, 128-130, 134

TIAA-CREF, 133-134, 254

V

Vanguard Group, 108

Variable annuity, 26-28, 31, 35, 38, 44-45, 58, 67, 73, 81, 83, 85, 88, 91, 100-101, 103-108, 112, 120-122, 126, 131, 139, 143, 147, 154, 158, 161, 166-167, 180, 189, 194, 196, 206-207, 223, 226-228, 246, 266, 269, 274, 280

Vesting, 29, 119, 280

W

Withdrawal, 29-30, 50, 54, 59, 64, 74, 119, 127, 136-137, 155, 169, 171, 178-179, 217, 227-228, 250, 268, 273-274, 276

Wrap fee, 100